Mary
Mother of Jesus

Mary
Mother of Jesus

Bruce E. Dana

ISBN 13: 978-1-4621-1042-1

Published by CFI, an imprint of Cedar Fort, Inc.
2373 W. 700 S., Springville, UT, 84663
Distributed by Cedar Fort, Inc., www.cedarfort.com

The Library of Congress has cataloged the hardcover edition as follows:

Dana, Bruce E.
Mary, Mother of Jesus / by Bruce E. Dana
> p. cm.
Includes bibliographical references.
ISBN 1-55517-557-0 (alk. paper)
1. Mary, Blessed Virgin, Saint. 2. Church of Jesus Christ of Latter-day Saints--Doctrines. I. Title
BX8643.M37 2001

2001003919

Cover design by Rebecca Greenwood
Cover design © 2012 by Lyle Mortimer
Typeset by Virginia Reeder

Printed in the United States of America

10 9 8 7 6 5 4 3 2 1

Printed on acid-free paper

Acknowledgments

To my wife Brenda, and my sons, Benjamin and Nathan, I express my love and appreciation; especially for allowing me time to research and write this work. Likewise, I express my love and appreciation to my parents, Edward K. and P. Shirley Dana, and my sister, Evelyn Giles, and my six daughters, Janalene, Connie, Michelle, Tami, Heather, and Brooke, for their constant love and devotion.

I am especially grateful for Lee Nelson and Lyle Mortimer of Cedar Fort, Inc., for their confidence in publishing this labor of love, titled, *Mary, Mother of Jesus.* Likewise, for publishing my first book, *Mysteries of the Kingdom.* I truly appreciate the staff of Cedar Fort—especially for their friendship and professional help in performing all of the necessary details that produce a professional and marketable product.

In writing this work, I am very grateful for my dear friend, Dennis "C" Davis, who, for thirty years, has generously shared his vast knowledge of the gospel with me. Regarding this work, I greatly appreciate his constructive criticism and helpful insights. Other trusted friends, Elder Robert L. Backman, John Brockbank, James Peterson, Donald Speth, Vaughn Cook, and Jean Britt, have read all or portions of my manuscript and have given valuable comments and recommendations. I am very appreciative of my mother-in-law, Barbara Jo (Jody) Lamb, who has carefully read my final manuscript and made helpful suggestions.

I express my deepest respect for Elders Bruce R. McConkie and James E. Talmage, and the scholars Alfred Edersheim and Frederic W. Farrar. The reader will gain a greater understanding of Mary because of the inspired writings of these gifted authors.

In particular, I am indebted to Mary, the mortal mother of Jesus Christ. I sincerely pray that I have portrayed her life as accurately as possible. In conclusion, I declare that Mary truly was a precious and chosen vessel.

CONTENTS

PREFACE

Alma, who is the son of Alma, reveals this truth about the mother of Jesus:

> "And behold, he shall be born of Mary, at Jerusalem which is the land of our forefathers, she being a virgin, a precious and chosen vessel, who shall be overshadowed and conceive by the power of the Holy Ghost, and bring forth a son, yea, even the Son of God." (Alma 7:10.)

Mary truly was a precious and chosen vessel. Due to her valiancy in the premortal existence, she was chosen to provide a physical body for our Lord. On earth, no other woman will experience the joys and challenges that she had. Using information from the scriptures, and recognized scholars, this work will portray her life as accurately as possible.

Due to the Bible being an abridgment of great and sacred events, there are only small glimpses of known facts recorded regarding our Savior, and of his mother, Mary. Silence is often prevalent in the scriptures regarding numerous personal matters. Notwithstanding, it is pleasing that we have been allowed to know what we do of the association and conversations between Jesus and his beloved mother.

In addition to more closely observing the social and personal characteristics of the Son of God and his mother, in the Jewish culture, it is most rewarding that we are allowed, to some degree, to understand their spiritual characteristics as well.

This work will not be a biography but more of a commentary and analysis of known events and actual conversations spoken and recorded in the New Testament. Due to the limited and abridged knowledge we have of Mary, a true biography cannot be written of her or even attempted. The reader should be aware that every commentary, including this work, will contain a certain amount of opinion and speculation. No biography or commentary can totally avoid this.

Whenever a General Authority is quoted in this work, it is the right and responsibility of the reader to compare those quoted expressions with the scriptures found in the four Standard Works of the Church, the words of the prophets, and official declarations issued by the First Presidency of the Church of Jesus Christ of Latter-day Saints. Then, through personal study and prayer, the reader can determine if the leading brethrens' statements are their own opinion or inspired words of truth.

The reader is informed that a portion of this work will have the same information and wording that is contained in the author's book, *Mysteries of the Kingdom*. Both books contain doctrines that pertain to, and give explanation about, Mary and her sacred calling to be the mother of our Lord.

CHAPTER ONE

MARY, A JEWISH MAIDEN

It was necessary that the mortal mother of Jesus Christ be born at a certain time and in a certain geographical location. By divine providence, she was raised a Jew, in the city of Nazareth of Galilee, two thousand years ago, and took upon herself physical features similar to her premortal spirit.[1] (Matt. 2:23; Luke 1:26-30; 1 Ne. 11:13; D&C 77:2)

PREMORTAL EXISTENCE

Prior to her mortal birth, Mary lived in a spirit realm known as the premortal existence. The Lord has not revealed how long she—and each of us—lived in this place; evidently, it was for a very long time.[2] While there, she developed and earned special talents and abilities.

"THE GREATEST FEMALE SPIRIT"

Due to her valiancy in keeping the teachings and commandments of God, Mary was selected above all female spirits assigned to this earth and foreordained to become the mortal mother of our Lord. To help us better understand her spiritual status, we will use the words of Elder Bruce R. McConkie:

> "Can we speak too highly of her whom the Lord has blessed above all women? There was only one Christ, and there is only one Mary. Each was noble and great in the preexistence, and each was foreordained to the ministry he or she performed. We cannot but think that the Father would choose the greatest female spirit to be the mother of his Son, even as he chose the male spirit like unto him to be the Savior..."[3]

MARY AND EVE

In view of Eve being the first woman on earth, and the mother of all living (Moses 4:26; 1 Ne. 5:11), and Mary being the mother of our Lord, a person may wonder who of the two was the greater in the premortal life? To help answer this question, we again rely upon the wisdom and logic of our apostolic scholar:

> "In my judgment, Mary is the number one woman who has ever lived on earth; she is the spirit daughter of God our Father, who was chosen to provide a body for his Son, who was to be born after the manner of the flesh...
>
> "I rate Eve as the number two woman among all of those who have or will come to earth. She, as the mother of all living, set the pattern for all future mothers with reference to bringing up their children in light and truth. She received all the blessings of the gospel, enjoyed the gifts of the Spirit, and sought to prepare her posterity for like blessings...
>
> "Now, from this point there is no order of priority. I have no reservation in acclaiming Mary as the number one woman of the earth and Eve as the number two."[4]

MARY WAS BORN ON EARTH

It needs to be emphasized that Mary came into this world bringing with her the talents, gifts, abilities, and spiritual endowments that she earned in abundance and developed in the premortal existence.

After this Jewish maiden was born on earth, her parents gave her the name that was revealed years earlier to holy men of God. That special name was Mary. (Mosiah 3:8; Alma 7:10.)

Her earthly parents cared and provided for her temporal and spiritual needs. As Mary grew, she was taught to be mannerly, well-groomed, virtuous, and a responsible and productive person. Further, this Jewish maiden was taught the law of Moses, as well as the prophecies of the Promised Messiah. Because of her domestic and religious training in the home, Mary believed in God, had faith and religious hope in his teachings, and lived his holy commandments. With a combination of her premortal nature, and the religious training she received in mortality, Mary rapidly learned the commandments of God and willingly conformed her life accordingly. Mary truly was a precious and chosen vessel. (Alma 7:10)

We will now learn why Mary was placed in a Jewish family instead of a Gentile family.

CHAPTER TWO

MARY WAS PLACED IN A JEWISH FAMILY

JEWISH AND GENTILE FAMILIES

To better understand why our Father in Heaven placed Mary in a Jewish family instead of a Gentile family, we turn to the eminent scholar, Alfred Edersheim[5] for information:

> "Education begins in the home, and there were not homes like those in Israel; it is imparted by influence and example, before it comes by teaching...What Jewish fathers and mothers were; what they felt towards their children; and with what reverence, affection, and care the latter [the child] returned [to the parents]...is known to every reader of the Old Testament.
>
> "...a religious atmosphere surrounded the child of Jewish parents..." (*The Life and Times of Jesus the Messiah. Book* 1:227)

Later in his writing, he gives this insight:

> "It was, indeed, no idle boast that the Jews 'were from their swaddling-clothes...trained to recognise [sic] God as their Father, and as the Maker of the world;' that, 'having been taught the knowledge (of the laws) from earliest youth, they bore in their souls the image of the commandments;' that 'from their earliest consciousness

they learned the laws, so as to have them, as it were, engraven upon the soul'...." (Ibid. 230)

To illustrate the difference between Jewish and Gentile children with those of their parents, Dr. Edersheim has penned:

> "The Gentile world here presented terrible contrast, alike in regard to the relation of parents and children, and the character and moral object of their upbringing." (Ibid. 226-227)

THE JEWS IN JESUS' DAY

In conjunction with Dr. Edersheim, and with more clarification, we turn to a writing of Elder Bruce R. McConkie:

> "The law of family worship, the system revealed by the Great Jehovah to enable his people to gain exaltation through the continuation of the family unit in eternity, was known, in part at least, to the Jews of Jesus' day and in the true sense of the word to no other Old World people. Jewish families, therefore, had a religious foundation and a spiritual status totally unknown among the Gentiles...such families lived lives of decency and morality. Husbands and wives were faithful to each other, scriptural study and daily prayer were part of the rituals of life, and the family members lived honest, sober, and upright lives...
>
> "In contrast, family life among the Gentiles was defiled, corrupt, devoid of decency, and of such a low order as scarcely to be worthy of the name..."[6]

Quoting from another of Edersheim's books,[7] Elder McConkie provides this information:

> "'Strange as it may sound,' Edersheim says, 'it is strictly true that, beyond the boundaries of Israel, it would be scarcely possible to speak with any propriety of family life, or even the family, as we understand these terms...'"[8]

In conclusion, as it pertains to the Jews as a whole nation, Elder McConkie gives this explanation:

> "True, their knowledge was incomplete, and the full glory of perfect familial relationships had been lost among them. But they had been born in the family of Israel; the traditions of their fathers still lingered in their homes; and they did have the holy scriptures, wherein the Abrahamic covenant and the chosen status of Israel were extolled. They were, indeed, a unique people, a peculiar people, a people set apart from all others. Their family-centered way of life, their religious traditions, their social customs all combined to separate them, to make them a people without peer..."[9]

Regarding our Lord, we read these words:

> "As we view Jewish families and Gentile families, is it any wonder that the Son of God came among the Jews? Though they would take his life in due course, because of priestcraft and iniquity, yet divine providence required an environment and a social and religious climate that would enable him to grow to maturity, unstained, preserved physically and spiritually, so that he could do his appointed work before he laid down his life as our Savior

and Redeemer."[10]

MARY'S APPOINTED WORK

In conjunction with what Elder McConkie has written of our Savior, we know that Mary was also required to be raised in that same "environment." She was raised in a Jewish family so that she could do her "appointed work." Her glorious yet challenging work was to be the mortal mother of our Lord.

Next, let us find out about Mary's educational process.

NOTES

1. Alfred Edersheim was a scholar, holding three higher educational degrees, M.A., D.D., PH.D. He was an author over one hundred years past, who accepted Jesus Christ as the literal Son of God.

In *The Mortal Messiah* series, Elder McConkie has periodically quoted Edersheim. In addition, Elder McConkie has written praising words of this religious man—*See* Book 1, pp. 130-131, and Book 4, p. 425, note 3.

CHAPTER THREE

MARY'S EDUCATIONAL PROCESS

THE PARENT'S ROLE

Being a unique people, Jewish parents taught and educated their children in Jewish practices as well as in the law of Moses; first by example, then by instruction. To assist us on how Mary, Joseph, and other Jewish children were educated, we will use the pattern as outlined by Dr. Edersheim:

JEWISH MOTHERS

"The first education was necessarily the mother's."[11] In speaking of mothers, most will agree that this singular person's influence and instruction will leave a lasting impression upon a child. Whether for good or bad, a mother's example and instruction shapes the destiny and thoughts of every child. It is true that every child is born with its own unique personality and temperament; however, while still young and impressionable, it is the mother who can influence her child to become better or worse. As it pertains to Mary, we can assume that in addition to her special, premortal nature, this young Jewish girl had a loving and caring mother who helped her become the best she could be.

Writing of the duties of a typical Jewish mother, our scholar explains:

> "...other religious duties devolved exclusively upon them. The Sabbath meal, the kindling of the Sabbath lamp, and the setting apart a portion of the dough from the bread for the household..."[12]

Even in our modern day, wherein many men are doing more domestic chores in the home, it is generally women who are the homemakers. Back in Jesus' day, and especially on the Sabbath, the homemaking duties were exclusively the mother's responsibility.

Continuing again with the role of a Jewish mother in educating her child, we learn this information:

> "...Even before he [the child] could follow her in such religious household duties, his eyes must have been attracted by the Mezuzah attached to the doorpost..."[13]

The Mezuzah was a little folded parchment, and on this parchment was "the name of the Most High" [God], and it "was reverently touched by each who came or went"...into the home..." In popular opinion it was the symbol of the Divine guard over Israel's homes..." Further, "...the duty of the Mezuzah was incumbent on women also..."[14]

From watching her mother, Mary learned these household duties and responsibilities. Then, when she became the mother of Jesus, she performed these same domestic chores.

JEWISH FATHERS

Turning our attention away from Jewish mothers, we gather the following information about Jewish fathers:

> "...it was the father who was 'bound to teach his

son'...the...knowledge of the Torah[15]... Directly [when] the child learned to speak, his religious instruction was to begin...with such verses of Holy Scripture...short prayers, and select sayings of the sages.[16] Very early the child must have been taught...some verse of Scripture beginning, or ending with, or at least containing, the same letters as his Hebrew name... The earliest hymns taught would be the Psalms..."[17]

TEACHINGS IN JEWISH HOMES

In Jewish homes, the law of Moses was taught and observed by all. From what has been written by Dr. Edersheim and Elder McConkie, we learn that both Mary and Joseph were taught and educated by the same parental process. Likewise, when this couple became the mother and foster father of Jesus, they began his educational process in the same manner.

Together, let us learn of the formal education of Jewish children, which included Mary and Joseph.

CHAPTER FOUR

FORMAL INSTRUCTION AND SCHOOLING

Concerning the formal education of Jewish children, which included Mary and Joseph, we rely once again upon Edersheim for information:

> "The regular instruction commenced with the fifth or sixth year (according to strength), when every child was sent to school. There can be no reasonable doubt that at that time such schools existed throughout the land..." Later in this same chapter, Dr. Edersheim further writes, "Suffice it that, from the teaching of the alphabet or of writing, onwards to the farthest limit of instruction in the most advanced Academies of the Rabbis, all is marked by extreme care, wisdom, accuracy, and a moral and religious purpose as the ultimate object."[18]

As it relates to the respective studies according to age, we gain this knowledge:

> "Roughly classifying the subjects of study, it was held, that, up to ten years of age, the Bible exclusively should be the text-book; from ten to fifteen the Mishnah, or traditional law; after that age, the student should enter on those theological discussions which occupied time and

> attention in the higher Academies of the Rabbis. Not that this progression would always be made."[19]

In conclusion, Edersheim has written these words of truth:

> "The teaching in school would, of course, be greatly aided by the services of the Synagogue, and the deeper influences of home-life."[20]

From this information, three things can be concluded: First, these unique people began their formal schooling at age five or six, and completed it in their fifteenth year. Advanced studies were available, but not mandatory. Secondly, their studies were more of a religious nature than a secular one. As Edersheim has previously stated, "...all is marked by...a moral and religious purpose as the ultimate object." Thirdly, though not mentioned by Edersheim, we know that both from their instruction in school and the Bible, the Jews knew of the prophecies of the Promised Messiah, and looked forward for a Deliverer to "free them from personal and national bondage." On this subject, Elder McConkie has written these informative words:

DELIVERER

> "It comes, therefore, as no surprise to find that all Israel in the days of Jesus were looking for a temporal Deliverer, for a Messiah born in the lineage of Abraham and David, who, sitting on the throne of their greatest king, would free them from personal and national bondage and vanquish their enemies. They looked for a pre-eminent Judahite ruler—for the scepter was not to depart

from David's Judah until Shiloh came—who would throw off the Roman yoke and scatter the legions of the Caesars.

"Such a Deliverer, such a Messiah, as they envisioned, would not only restore the kingdom to Israel, but would also return the dispersed of that great nation to their original inheritance in their promised Canaan."[21]

From her religious training in the home, and in the classroom, Mary knew of and prayed for the fulfillment of the "Deliverer" when Gabriel appeared to her and announced that she was to be the mother of the Son of God. It is also reasonable to believe that due to the veil of forgetfulness that was drawn over her mind of her premortal life, prior to God's messenger being sent to her, Mary did not know that she would be a key person in bringing to pass the literal fulfillment of these prophecies.

MARY GREW IN WISDOM AND STATURE

With a combination of her premortal nature, as well as the parental teachings in her Jewish home, and those in the formal Jewish school, this Jewish girl was specifically being brought up to raise Jesus. Similarly, what is written so well of her young, divine Son, can also be written of her:

> "And [Mary] increased in wisdom and stature, and in favour [sic] with God and man." (Luke 2:52)

Regarding Mary, let us find out about her physical characteristics.

NOTES

1. Dr. Edersheim has written:

The study of the Bible commenced with that of the Book of Leviticus. Thence it passed to the other parts of the Pentateuch; then to the Prophets; and, finally, to the Hagiographa. What now constitutes the Gemara or Talmud was taught in the Academies, to which access could not be gained till after the age of fifteen. Care was taken not to send a child too early to school, nor to overwork him when there. For this purpose the school-hours were fixed, and attendance shortened during the summer months. (Edersheim 1:232)

2. Pentateuch is known as the first five books of the Old Testament. The Prophets are known as historical books like Joshua, Judges, 1, 2 Samuel, and 1, 2 Kings. The Hagiographa consists of the third of the three ancient Jewish divisions of the Old Testament, containing those books not in the Law (Torah) or the Prophets and usually include the Psalms, Proverbs, Job, the Song of Solomon, Ruth, Lamentations, Ecclesiastes, Esther, Daniel, Ezra, Nehemiah, and Chronicals. The Gemara is the second part of the Talmud, consisting chiefly of commentary of the Mishnah. The Mishnah is the first section of the Talmud, a compilation of early oral interpretations of the scriptures dating from about 200 A.D.

CHAPTER FIVE

PHYSICAL CHARACTERISTICS OF MARY

NEPHI'S VISION OF MARY

The Lord has revealed that the premortal spirit that is housed in the mortal body is "in the likeness of that which is temporal." (D&C 77:2)[22] Accordingly, Mary took upon herself physical characteristics that are similar to her premortal spirit.

Nearly six hundred years prior to the birth of Christ, a Nephite prophet, whose name is Nephi, was privileged to see Mary in vision. From this blessed man, we read of her physical attractiveness:

> "For it came to pass after I had desired to know the things that my father had seen, and believing that the Lord was able to make them known unto me,...I was caught away in the Spirit of the Lord, yea, into an exceedingly high mountain...
>
> "And it came to pass that I looked and beheld the great city of Jerusalem, and also other cities. And I beheld the city of Nazareth; and in the city of Nazareth I beheld a virgin, and she was exceedingly fair and white.
>
> "...and an angel came down and stood before me; and he said unto me: Nephi, what beholdest thou?
>
> "And I said unto him: A virgin, most beautiful and fair above all other virgins." (1 Ne. 11:1-15)

"FAIR"

According to a dictionary definition, the word fair means: Pleasing to the eye, flawless quality, and clean and pure. Was this not an appropriate description of Mary?

Continuing with the scriptural account, the angel told Nephi who this attractive woman was:

> "And he said unto me: Behold, the virgin whom thou seest is the mother of the Son of God, after the manner of the flesh.
>
> "And it came to pass that I beheld that she [Mary] was carried away in the Spirit; and after she had been carried away in the Spirit for the space of a time the angel spake unto me, saying: Look!
>
> "And I looked and beheld the virgin again, bearing a child in her arms.
>
> "And the angel said unto me: Behold the Lamb of God, yea, even the Son of the Eternal Father!" (1 Ne. 11:18-21)

"PLEASING PERSONALITY"

From this revealed knowledge, are we amiss to say that besides being physically attractive, Mary's personality and spiritual countenance were equally pleasing? Beauty is more than just physical. It also encompasses a variety of things such as the following: a warm personality, an unassuming and caring nature, a reverent and spiritual attitude, a special smile, honorable gestures of affection, and true goodness manifesting itself. Combining all of these traits, we may safely assume that besides being physically attractive, Mary also had a pleasing personality.

What of Mary's immediate family? Let us discover what has been revealed on this subject.

CHAPTER SIX

MARY'S IMMEDIATE FAMILY

With the limited amount of knowledge that is revealed, we are not informed of the number of individuals in Mary's immediate family. However, by a careful reading of one scripture, found in the Gospel of John, we discover that this Jewish maiden had at least one sister.

> "Now there stood by the cross of Jesus his mother, *and his mother's sister*, Mary the wife of Cleophas, and Mary Magdalene." (John 19:25—Italics added)

Regarding this scripture, Elder James E. Talmage has written these informative words:

> "From the fact that John mentions the mother of Jesus and 'his mother's sister' (John 19:25) and omits mention of Salome by name, some expositors [Those individuals who expound or explain] hold that Salome was the sister of Mary the mother of Jesus; and therefore the Savior's aunt. This relationship would make James and John cousins to Jesus. While the scriptural record does not disprove this alleged kinship, it certainly does not affirm the same."[23]

SALOME, THE SISTER OF MARY

Let us consider another point of view. Analyzing two New Testament scriptures, which speak of the mother of Zebedee's children and the woman called Salome, the reader can formulate who was the mother of James and John.

> "Among which was Mary Magdalene, and Mary the mother of James and Joses, and *the mother of Zebedee's children*." (emphasis added) (Matt. 27:56)

> "There were also women looking on afar off: among whom was Mary Magdalene, and Mary the mother of James the less and of Joses, and *Salome*;" (emphasis added) (Mark 15:40)

As it pertains to Mary, and her sister, Dr. Edersheim has written these declarative words:

> "Thus Salome, the wife of Zebedee and St. John's mother, was the sister of the Virgin, and the beloved disciple the cousin (on the mother's side) of Jesus, and the nephew of the Virgin. This also helps to explain why the care of the Mother had been entrusted to him."[24]

In harmony with Edersheim's statement, Elder McConkie assuredly and without reservation has written:

> "Jesus' attention is now turned to a scene of sorrow and despair. By the cross stands his mother...With her are three other faithful women—her sister, Salome, the wife of Zebedee and the mother of James and John (who thus were cousins of Jesus), Mary the wife of Cleophas; and Mary Magdalene."[25]

Therefore, as it relates to Mary and her sister, Salome, our loving Father in Heaven placed each of these noble and great ladies—just as he did Jesus—in a Jewish home, in order to prepare each to "grow to maturity, unstained, preserved physically and spiritually," in order that individually and collectively they could do their "appointed work." Mary's work was to be the mother of Jesus. Salome's work was to be the mother of James and John, who in turn became apostolic witnesses of their first cousin and Lord. (Wording taken from note 10, pp. 7-8)

Mary and Joseph were a special couple. Let us discover how and when they met.

CHAPTER SEVEN

MARY AND JOSEPH IN NAZARETH

Two thousand years ago, an event transpired that never has been or will ever again be duplicated on this earth. That glorious occurrence was a heavenly announcement to a Jewish maiden, living in Nazareth, that she was to be the mother of "the Son of God." (*See* Luke 1:26-35)

NAZARETH OF GALILEE

Regarding the "city of Galilee, named Nazareth" (Luke 1:26), we learn that this small town was located in one of three regions located in Palestine. The region farthest north was called Galilee. From various descriptions, we understand that this particular region covered a land area of approximately thirty miles by sixty. Further, that "...the Galilee of the time of Jesus was not only of the richest fertility, cultivated to the utmost, and thickly covered with populous towns and villages, but the [center] of every known industry, and the busy road of the world's commerce."[26]

From this description, we can visualize that people from all walks of life, and business, traveled to and from the towns of Palestine, including that of Nazareth. Relying exclusively upon the knowledge of Alfred Edersheim, we can more fully understand the characteristics of this Jewish town:

"Nazareth nestling on the breast of the mountain, the eye would rest on a scene of tranquil, homely beauty. Just outside the town, in the northwest, bubbled the spring or well, the trysting-spot [meeting place] of towns-people, and welcome resting-place of travellers.[sic] Beyond it stretched lines of houses, each with its flat roof standing out distinctly against the clear sky; watered, terraced gardens, gnarled wide-spreading fig trees, graceful feathery palms, scented oranges, silvery olive trees, thick hedges, rich pasture land, then the bounding hills to the south; and beyond, the seemingly unbounded expanse of the wide plain of Esdraelon!

"And yet, withdrawn from the world...we must not think of it as a lonely village...

"...the quiet little town was not a stagnant pool of rustic seclusion. Men of all nations, busy with another life than that of Israel, would appear in the streets of Nazareth; and through them thoughts, associations, and hopes connected with the great outside world be stirred. But, on the other hand, Nazareth was also one of the great [centers] of Jewish Temple-life...

"We may take it, that the people of Nazareth were like those of other little towns...with all the peculiarities of the impulsive, straight-spoken, hot-blooded, brave, intensely national Galileans; with the deeper feelings and almost instinctive habits of thought and life, which were the outcome of long centuries of Old Testament training... The home-life would be all the purer... The purity of betrothal in Galilee was less likely to be sullied, and weddings were more simple than in Judaea... The bride was chosen, not as in Judaea, where money was too often the motive...

"Such a home was that to which Joseph was about to

bring the maiden, to whom he had been betrothed..."[27]

HOW AND WHEN MARY AND JOSEPH MET

To assist us in determining when and how Mary and Joseph met, fell in love, and made the important and sacred decision to marry, we turn to the genealogies recorded in the New Testament. The Apostle Matthew records one lineage (1:1-16); the Apostle Luke presents another lineage. (3:23-38) Matthew writes that "Jacob begat Joseph the husband of Mary, of whom was born Jesus..." (1:16) Luke writes that "Jesus...(as was supposed) [was] the son of Joseph, which was the son of Heli." (3:23) To help determine who the father of Joseph was, we again turn to Elder Bruce R. McConkie for clarification. With the guidance of our apostolic scholar, we not only find the identity of Joseph's father, but also the true meaning of the lineages recorded in the Gospels of Matthew and Luke:

> "Matthew identifies his Gospel as 'The book of the generation of Jesus Christ, the son of David, the son of Abraham.' Then he gives a genealogy down to 'Joseph the husband of Mary, of whom was born Jesus, who is called Christ.' Luke begins with this same Joseph and traces the genealogy back to 'Adam, which was the son of God,' or, as the Joseph Smith Translation has it, to 'Adam, who was formed of God, and [was] the first man upon the earth.'
>
> "Matthew's and Luke's accounts seemingly do not agree, though, in fact, the two of them taken together give a perfect picture of what is involved. Both purport to give the genealogy of Joseph, whose bloodline is not involved, but who was of the royal lineage. It is generally agreed that

> Matthew's account gives the royal lineage and therefore records names of those whose right it was to sit on David's throne, and that Luke's record contains the personal pedigree of Mary's husband. Matthew says that Joseph was the son of Jacob, and Luke says that he was the son of Heli. *It appears, however, that Jacob and Heli were brothers and that Heli was the father of Joseph and Jacob the father of Mary*, making Joseph and Mary first cousins with the same ancestral lines. How fitting it is that the New Testament should preserve both a royal and a personal pedigree of these two, so that there could be no question, either by blood or by kingly right, as to the noble and exalted status of the Son of David. 'Had Judah been a free and independent nation, ruled by her rightful sovereign, Joseph the carpenter would have been her crowned king; and his lawful successor to the throne would have been Jesus of Nazareth, the King of the Jews.' (Talmage, p. 87—Italics added)"[28]

From this information, the reader can safely formulate that from the time of their early infancy, Mary and Joseph knew one another well and associated together often for two apparent reasons: First, they were first cousins on their fathers' side. Secondly, these two people and their parental families lived in the same town of Nazareth. From the scriptural record, we know that when Gabriel appeared to Mary, she was living in her parents' home. (Luke 1:26-28) Joseph was also living in Nazareth, and made a living as a carpenter. (Matt. 13:55; Mark 6:3) We also know that Mary and Joseph were married in Nazareth, and they lived in this town. To support this statement, we read that prior to the birth of Jesus, both Joseph and Mary "went up from Galilee, out of the city of Nazareth, into Judaea, unto the city of David, which is called Bethlehem..."

(Luke 2:4)

Due to their close and frequent association, Mary and Joseph knew the goodness and quality of each. And, similar with millions of couples who meet and do things together often, Joseph and Mary fell in love and wanted to spend their remaining lives as husband and wife.

If indeed they were first cousins, some individuals may believe it would have been inappropriate for Mary and Joseph to marry. In response to that belief, it is important to know that during this era there was no stigma associated with or physiological concerns regarding relatives, such as first cousins, marrying one another. Accordingly, being in love, when Joseph asked Mary to marry him, she readily consented.

Let us learn what has been written about Mary's and Joseph's probable marital ages.

CHAPTER EIGHT

PROBABLE MARITAL AGES OF MARY AND JOSEPH

As with numerous personal matters, the Gospel writers have not revealed the marital ages of Mary and Joseph. However, from Frederic W. Farrar,[29] Dr. Edersheim, and Elder McConkie, we can determine their ages fairly accurately.

From Farrar, we discover that there were certain duty requirements of male members of the Jewish race which were determined according to their ages:

> "According to Juda Ben Tema, at five he was to study the Scriptures (Mikra), at ten the Mishna, at thirteen the Talmud; at eighteen he was to marry, at twenty to acquire riches, at thirty, strength, at forty, prudence, and so on to the end."[30]

In almost the same order, Dr. Edersheim has penned similar expressions. Pertaining to the marital age of a Jewish man, our scholar has written: "...at eighteen years, marriage..."[31]

Therefore, from these noted scholars of over a hundred years past, it appears that the standard age of a Jewish man to marry was at or around eighteen.

Throughout *The Mortal Messiah* series, Elder Bruce R. McConkie quotes from both Edersheim and Farrar. Accordingly, the reader can more fully understand why our apostolic scholar has written these words:

> "Men married at sixteen or seventeen years of age, almost never later than twenty; and women at a somewhat younger age, often when not older than fourteen. These ages applied to all, Joseph and Mary included."[32]

Regarding Joseph, Elder McConkie has written these declarative words:

> "The common concept...that Joseph was an old man when he took Mary as his bride is patently false. This traditional notion arises from two things: (1)The fact that Joseph apparently had died by the time of the crucifixion; at least on that occasion our Lord asked the Beloved Disciple to care for Mary...(John 19:25-27) (2)False traditions which maintain that Mary was a virgin forever, had no sexual association with Joseph, and bore him no children. The only logical circumstances under which Joseph could have been substantially older than Mary would have been one in which he was taking her as a second wife after the death of a previous spouse, or one in which he and Mary were entering into a polygamous marriage. As Edersheim says: 'Polygamy...undoubtedly was in force at the time of our Lord.' (Temple, p. 142) There is no reason to believe that either of these conditions prevailed, and we are left to conclude that Joseph was certainly not older than twenty years when he took Mary as his wife, and she was at least fourteen, perhaps fifteen or sixteen."[33]

In conclusion, from what has been written by these noted scholars, it appears that Mary and Joseph were married in, or near, their teen years. As most people will agree, maturity is not always associated with chronological age. Notwithstanding Mary's young age, it is reasonable to believe that due to her great calling to be the mother of our Lord, she was quite mature. Likewise, the same belief applies to Joseph being the foster father of Jesus. We will now learn about the betrothal of Mary and Joseph.

NOTES

1. Frederic W. Farrar, an eminent scholar, of the Church of England, with the titles of D.D. and F.R.S., was an author, over a hundred years past, who is noted for his literary talents and knowledge of the scriptures.

Elder Bruce R. McConkie, in his series, *The Mortal Messiah: From Bethlehem to Calvary*, has quoted frequently from the writings of Mr. Farrar. In addition, he has written praising words of this talented man—*See* Book 4, pp.180-181; page 425, note 2.

CHAPTER NINE

BETROTHAL OF MARY AND JOSEPH

Quoting from another author, Cunningham Geikie, Elder James E. Talmage gives this explanation about a betrothal in "Mary's day:"

> "Among the Jews of Mary's day it was even more of an actual engagement... The betrothal was formally made with rejoicings in the house of the bride under a tent or slight canopy raised for the purpose. It was called the 'making sacred' as the bride thenceforth was sacred to her husband in the strictest sense. To make it legal, the bridegroom gave his betrothed a piece of money, or the worth of it, before witnesses, with the words, 'Lo, thou art betrothed unto me,' or by a formal writing in which similar words and the maiden's name were given, and this in the same way was handed to her before witnesses."[34]

Specifically speaking of Mary and Joseph, Dr. Edersheim has written these words:

> "But at the time of their betrothal, alike Joseph and Mary were extremely poor, as appears—not indeed from his [sic] being a carpenter, since a trade was regarded as almost a religious duty—but from the offering at the presentation of Jesus in the Temple. Accordingly, their

betrothal must have been the simplest, and the dowry settled the smallest possible. Whichever of the two modes of betrothal may have been adopted: in the presence of witnesses—either by solemn word of mouth, in due prescribed formality, with the added pledge of a piece of money, however small, or of money's worth for use; or else by writing...there would be no sumptuous [expensive] feast to follow; and the ceremony would conclude with some such benediction as that afterwards in use: 'Blessed art Thou, O Lord our God, King of the World, Who hath sanctified us by His Commandments...' From that moment Mary was the betrothed wife of Joseph; their relationship as sacred, as if they had already been wedded. Any breach of it would be treated as adultery; nor could the bond be dissolved except, as after marriage, by regular divorce. Yet months might intervene between the betrothal and marriage."[35]

GABRIEL VISITED MARY

The scriptural record is silent on the day and time that this heavenly manifestation transpired. What we do know is that while alone in the home of her parents, Mary was visited by a heavenly messenger from God, by the name of Gabriel. From the Prophet Joseph Smith, we learn that Gabriel was known in mortality as Noah.[36]

In her home, and with respect, the angel declares, "Hail, thou that art highly favoured, the Lord is with thee: blessed art thou among women.

"And when she saw him, she was troubled at his saying, and cast in her mind what manner of salutation this should be." (Luke 1:28-29—Italics added)

Is it any wonder why Mary was "troubled" by Gabriel's appearance and greeting? Knowing of her feelings and concerns, this heavenly messenger spoke these calming and informative words:

> "...Fear not, Mary: for thou hast found favour with God.
>
> "And, behold, thou shalt conceive in thy womb, and bring forth a son, and shalt call his name JESUS.
>
> "He shall be great, and shall be called the Son of the Highest...." (Luke 1:30-32)

Imagine what Mary was experiencing by this heavenly manifestation. Rarely does an angel appear to individuals on earth. Then, compound this spiritual experience by the surprising announcement that she was to be the mother of the "Son of the Highest."

MARY'S RESPONSE

Regarding her response, we turn to the expressions of Elder James E. Talmage for understanding:

> "Even yet she comprehended but in part the import of this momentous visitation. Not in the spirit of doubt such as had prompted Zacharias to ask for a sign, but through an earnest desire for information and explanation, Mary, conscious of her unmarried status and sure of her virgin condition, asked: 'How shall this be, seeing I know not a man?'"[37]

GABRIEL

Gabriel, as clearly and as plainly as he can, explained to Mary:

> "...The Holy Ghost shall come upon thee, and the power of the Highest shall overshadow thee: therefore also that holy thing [child] which shall be born of thee shall be called the Son of God." (Luke 1:35)

Then, he told this Jewish maiden of her cousin Elisabeth's condition. (*See* Luke 1:36-37)

Mary responded with gentle submissiveness and humble acceptance[38] "...Behold the handmaid of the Lord; be it unto me according to thy word." (Luke 1:38) The record states that after Mary spoke these humble and obedient words, Gabriel departed. Now alone, Mary was left to ponder, and wait, for the angel's words to be fulfilled.

Regarding spiritual experiences, only those individuals who have had one know of the difficulty in explaining it to others, and having them properly understand. Only by the Spirit can spiritual experiences be expressed and understood. In Mary's case with Gabriel, divine wisdom mandated discreet silence. Eventually, there would be a time and a place for her to share it. For now, no one, including her betrothed Joseph, would know of this manifestation.

Just as it was written regarding the birth of Jesus, this same statement was applicable to her experience with Gabriel: "But Mary kept all these things, and pondered them in her heart." (Luke 2:19)

AFTER GABRIEL'S DEPARTURE

We are not informed of the time between Gabriel's announcement to Mary and her entering into the presence of the Highest. All that we know is that it transpired shortly thereafter.

NOTES

1. Regarding Gabriel, the Prophet Joseph Smith has revealed:

"The priesthood was first given to Adam...He is Michael the Archangel, spoken of in the Scriptures. Then to Noah, who is Gabriel; he stands next in authority to Adam in the Priesthood; he was called of God to this office, and was the father of all living in this day, and to him was given the dominion. These men held keys first on earth, and then in heaven." (Joseph Fielding Smith, comp., *Teachings of the Prophet Joseph Smith.* 1938. p. 157. Italics added)

CHAPTER TEN

MARY WAS CARRIED AWAY IN THE SPIRIT

From Nephi, we learn an important truth regarding Mary and the conception of the Son of God. In vision, he saw "that she was carried away in the Spirit; and after she had been carried away in the Spirit for the space of a time...I...beheld the virgin again, bearing a child in her arms." (1 Ne. 11:19-20) The next verse reveals who the child was: "Behold the Lamb of God, yea, even the Son of the Eternal Father!" (1 Ne. 11: 21)

What does it mean to be carried away in the Spirit? To answer this question, we turn to this same Nephi and read of his own experience. Just prior to this man seeing Mary in vision, he writes these words:

> "For it came to pass after I had desired to know the things that my father had seen, and believing that the Lord was able to make them known unto me, as I sat pondering in mine heart I was caught away in the Spirit of the Lord, yea, into an exceedingly high mountain, which I never had before seen, and upon which I never had before set my foot." (1 Ne. 11:1)

Then, this insightful information is given:

> "And the Spirit said unto me: Behold, what desirest thou?

"And I said: I desire to behold the things which my father saw.

"...for I spake unto him as a man speaketh; for I beheld that he was in the form of a man; yet nevertheless, I knew that it was the Spirit of the Lord; and he spake unto me as a man speaketh with another." (1 Ne. 11:2,3, 11)

SPIRIT OF THE LORD

Turning our attention to this personage referred to as the "Spirit of the Lord," there are different opinions among members of the Church regarding the identity of this Spirit. Some believe it is the premortal Spirit Christ; others believe it is the Holy Ghost, who is a personage of Spirit. (*See* D&C 130:22) With faith, we trust the Lord will someday reveal the true identity of this Spirit personage who appeared to Nephi. Whether it was the Spirit Christ or the Holy Ghost, we know that this righteous man was bodily transported, by the Spirit, to a high mountain which he had neither seen nor visited. We know Nephi was bodily transported for he himself has written: "And upon the wings[39] of his Spirit hath my body been carried away upon exceedingly high mountains...." (2 Ne. 4:25; *see also* Ezek. 37:1; 1 Ne. 1:8)

MARY WAS BODILY TRANSPORTED

Citing the respective scriptural references, Elder McConkie has written that individually and at different times, Jesus, Ezekiel, Nephi, Mary, and the son of Helaman, named Nephi, and Philip were "transported bodily" from one place to another by the Spirit.[40]

From these documented experiences, we know that within a short time after Gabriel appeared to Mary, this chosen vessel was bodily transported from Nazareth into the presence of the Highest, either by the Spirit Christ or the Spirit personage called the Holy Ghost. Whether she was transported instantaneously or within seconds or minutes, we are left to wonder. What we do know is that one moment Mary was *physically* in Nazareth; another moment she was *physically* in the presence of God the Father.

OFFSPRING

Regarding offspring, Elder Melvin J. Ballard has explained this truth:

> "The nature of the offspring is determined by the nature of the substance that flows in the veins of the being. When blood flows in the veins of the being, the offspring will be what blood produces, which is tangible flesh and bone, but when that which flows in the veins is spirit matter, a substance which is more refined and pure and glorious than blood, the offspring of such beings will be spirit children."[41]

In harmony with this statement, we read these words by Charles W. Penrose, who was later ordained an Apostle and a counselor in the First Presidency:

> The resurrection: "The corruptible blood was purged from the veins [of Jesus Christ], and incorruptible spiritual fluid occupied its place. It was buried a natural body, it was resurrected a spiritual body."[42]

Because God the Father does not have blood running through his resurrected body, but spirit matter or spiritual fluid, the number of people who have lived or will yet live upon this earth are his spirit children.

The fluid that is circulated through human beings is called "blood." Blood being more heavy than spirit matter, we know that this is the predominant element in determining what type of offspring the premortal Christ would become in mortality.

MARY AND THE FATHER

From this information, we can more fully understand why Mary, who was a mortal being with blood flowing in her veins, was overshadowed by the Highest, an immortal being with "spirit matter" or "spiritual fluid" flowing through his veins, and that holy child of their sacred union would become the mortal Jesus Christ, with both fluids flowing in his veins. From his mother, our Lord inherited the ability to die physically because of the blood; from his Father, Christ inherited the power to live forever because of spiritual fluid. We know that when Jesus died on the cross, he said, "Father, into thy hands I commend my spirit: and having said thus, he [voluntarily] gave up the ghost." (Luke 23:46)

CONCEPTION OF THE SON OF GOD

Regarding Mary and the conception of the Son of God, Elder James E. Talmage has written these informative words:

> "That Child to be born of Mary was begotten of Elohim, the Eternal Father, not in violation of natural law but in accordance with a higher manifestation thereof; and, the offspring from that association of supreme sanc-

tity, celestial Sireship, and pure though mortal maternity, was of right to be called the 'Son of the Highest.'"43

There are many people who do not properly understand or accept as the truth that the conception of Jesus Christ was accomplished by a literal union between God the Father and the mortal Mary. With the Spirit as our guide, in the next four chapters, we will present doctrines that relate to this holy subject.

CHAPTER ELEVEN

THE GODHEAD IS MADE UP OF SEPARATE BEINGS

In addition to the supreme, intelligent God there are two other presiding beings which form the Godhead. "...these personages, according to Abraham's record, are called God the first, the Creator; God the second, the Redeemer; and God the third, the witness or Testator."[44] As Latter-day Saints, we know them better as "God, the Eternal Father, and...His Son, Jesus Christ, and...the Holy Ghost."[45] From Abraham's record and the teachings of the Prophet Joseph Smith, we know that three separate and distinct beings form the Godhead.

THE FATHER IS A RESURRECTED MAN

The Father is a glorified, resurrected man, the same as his resurrected and glorified Son. Regarding this subject, we turn our attention to the time when the resurrected Christ first appeared in the upper room to a number of faithful members, including ten of the Twelve Apostles. The reason only ten Apostles were present is as follows: (1)Judas Iscariot commited suicide after betraying our Lord. (Matt. 27:3-5) (2)For some unexplained reason, Thomas was not present. (John 20:24) With the doors closed and locked, "Jesus himself stood in the midst of them." These apostolic witnesses "were terrified and affrighted, and supposed that they had seen a spirit." Jesus spoke these assuring words, "Why are ye troubled? and why do thoughts arise in your hearts? Behold my hands and my feet, that it is I myself: handle me, and see; for a spirit hath not flesh and bones, as ye see me have." (Luke 24:37-39) A week later, Thomas was present with the ten apostles who had previously seen the risen Lord. Again, the Savior appeared and commanded his doubting Apostle to "Reach hither thy finger, and behold my hands; and reach hither thy hand, and thrust it into my side: and be not faithless, but believing." After obeying, Thomas no longer doubted that Jesus was resurrected and had a tangible body of flesh and bones. (John 20:26-29)

In both appearances, our resurrected Lord told his Apostles to look at his "hands" and to touch his person. Though Jesus is immortal, and can no longer die, he has all of his body parts and looks the same as he did as a mortal. The major difference is that blood no longer flows in his veins but spirit matter or spiritual fluid.[46]

We also understand from these recorded events that the expression "flesh and bones" is used to identify a resurrected, immortal being. In harmony with this expression, the Prophet Joseph Smith has revealed: "The Father has a body of flesh and bones as tangible as man's; the Son also; but the Holy Ghost has not a body of flesh and bones, but is a personage of Spirit." (D&C 130:22.)

From these scriptural references, we know that the Father, like his Son, is a glorified, resurrected Man. Further, that the Father and the Son have a physical body similar to mortal men. The major difference is the fluid flowing in their veins. Therefore, glorified and resurrected, the Highest was physically able to overshadow Mary and become the literal Father of his Son, Jesus Christ.

NATURALLY BEGOTTEN

What does it mean to be naturally begotten? To answer, we use expressions from three General Authorities. Elder Heber C. Kimball provides the following information:

> "I will say that I was naturally begotten; so was my father, and also my Saviour Jesus Christ. According to the Scriptures, he is the first begotten of his father in the flesh, and there was nothing unnatural about it."[47]

From President Brigham Young, we read:

> "The birth of the Saviour was as natural as are the births of our children; it was the result of natural action. He partook of flesh and blood—was begotten of his Father, as we were of our fathers."[48]

From Elder Bruce R. McConkie, we come to understand:

> "...Christ was begotten by an Immortal Father in the same way that mortal men are begotten by mortal fathers."[49]

Elder McConkie further writes:

> "...There is nothing figurative about his paternity; he was begotten, conceived and born in the normal and natural course of events, for he is the Son of God, and that designation means what it says."[50]

From these plainly spoken words, it should be clear that Jesus was begotten by his Heavenly Father in the same way that all men and women in mortality are begotten of their earthly parents. In addition, it should be clear also that the conception of Jesus Christ was the result of a literal union between God the Father and the precious and chosen vessel, Mary.

NOTES

1. "The blood he [Jesus Christ] spilled upon Mount Calvary he did not receive again into his veins. That was poured out, and when he was resurrected, another element took the place of the blood. It will be so with every person who receives a resurrection: the blood will not be resurrected with the body, being designed only to sustain the life of the present organization." (Brigham Young, *Journal of Discourses*, Volume 7, p. 163; June 5, 1859) (See *Mysteries of the Kingdom*, p. 63)

CHAPTER TWELVE

CLARIFICATION OF MATTHEW 1:18

From the Gospel of Matthew, the following information is given:

> "Now the birth of Jesus Christ was on this wise: When as his mother Mary was espoused to Joseph, before they came together, she was found with child of the Holy Ghost." (Matt. 1:18)

From Matthew's account it raises doubts whether Jesus was begotten by our Heavenly Father or was the child of the Holy Ghost. To understand the meaning of Matthew's account, we again turn to Elder McConkie for explanation and clarification:

> "Just as Jesus is literally the Son of Mary, so he is the personal and literal offspring of God the Eternal Father, who himself is an exalted personage having a tangible body of flesh and bones. (D&C 130:22.) Apostate religionists—unable to distinguish between the Father, Son, and Holy Ghost—falsely suppose that the Holy Ghost was the Father of our Lord. Matthew's statement, 'she was found with child of the Holy Ghost,' properly translated should say, 'she was found with child by the power of the Holy Ghost.' (Matt. 1:18.) Luke's account (Luke 1:35.) accurately records what took place. Alma perfectly describes our

> Lord's conception and birth by prophesying: Christ 'shall be born of Mary,...she being a virgin, a precious and chosen vessel, who shall be overshadowed and conceive by the power of the Holy Ghost, and bring forth a son, yea, even the Son of God.' (Alma 7:10.) Nephi spoke similarly when he said that at the time of her conception, Mary 'was carried away in the Spirit,' with the result that the child born of her was 'the Lamb of God, yea, even the Son of the Eternal Father.' (1 Ne. 11:19-21.) As Gabriel told Luke, he was the 'Son of the Highest' (Luke 1:32.), and 'the Highest' is the first member of the godhead, not the third."[51]

From this explanation, it should be clear that Jesus Christ is the offspring of God and Mary; not of the Holy Ghost and Mary. Further, it was by the sustaining power of the Holy Ghost that Mary was able to be in the presence of the Highest and not be consumed by his brightness and glory. (*See* Heb. 1:3; 2 Thes. 2:8; JS-H 1:15-17)

JESUS CHRIST WAS BORN OF A VIRGIN

The scriptures emphasize that Mary was a virgin. This includes the time before and after the birth of Jesus, until she was known by her husband, Joseph. (*See* Matt. 1:24-25) The question naturally arises, if indeed the Father and Mary conceived Jesus by a literal union, how can Mary remain a virgin? To answer this intriguing question, we turn once again to Elder Bruce R. McConkie for explanation:

> "Mary was a virgin...until after the birth of our Lord. Then, for the first time, she was known by Joseph, her husband; and other children, both sons and daughters,

> were then born to her. (Matt. 13:55-56; Mark 6:3; Gal 1:19.) She conceived and brought forth her Firstborn Son while yet a virgin because the Father of that child was an immortal personage."[52]

From this explanation, we learn that Mary's virginity was retained because of the fact that the conception of Jesus Christ was a union between a mortal woman and an Immortal Man. Mary ceased being a virgin when she was "known by Joseph, her husband" because that particular union was between a mortal man and a mortal woman. (Matt. 1:25)

CHAPTER THIRTEEN

JESUS CHRIST'S CONCEPTION WAS NOT DEGRADING

Some individuals may believe that if there were a literal union between the Father and Mary that this act would degrade God and debauch Mary. Elder Melvin J. Ballard gives this inspired explanation:

> "Mary told the story most beautifully when she said that an angel of the Lord came to her and told her that she had found favor in the sight of God, and had come to be worthy of the fulfillment of the promises heretofore made, to become the virgin mother of the Redeemer of the world. She afterwards, referring to the event, said: 'God hath done wonderful things unto me.' 'And the Holy Ghost came upon her,' is the story, 'and she came into the presence of the highest.' No man or woman can live in mortality and survive the presence of the Highest except by the sustaining power of the Holy Ghost. So it came upon her to prepare her for admittance into the divine presence, and the power of the Highest, who is the Father, was present, and overshadowed her, and the holy Child that was born of her was called the Son of God.
>
> "Men who deny this, or who think it degrades our Father, have no true conception of the sacredness of the most marvelous power with which God has endowed mortal men—the power of creation. Even though that

> power may be abused and may become a mere harp of pleasure to the wicked, nevertheless it is the most sacred and holy and divine function with which God has endowed man. Made holy, it is retained by the Father of us all, and in his exercise of that great and marvelous creative power and function, he did not debase himself, degrade himself, nor debauch Mary. Thus Christ became the literal Son of a divine Father, and no one else was worthy to be his father."[53]

From these inspired and enlightening words, we understand that mortals view the creative power differently than the Father, for as Isaiah has well written: "For my thoughts are not your thoughts, neither are your ways my ways, saith the Lord." (Isa. 55:8) Elder Ballard has explained it so plainly, yet powerfully, that the creative power is the most sacred, holy, and divine function that can be performed by man and God.

God the Father is the most holy, righteous, and pure-minded Man of all men. Further, he has the most respect for women and womanhood above all others. When Mary was in his presence and he overshadowed her, he performed a most sacred and holy function, with divine tenderness, love, and respect. Thereby, he did not degrade or debase himself or Mary.

This most righteous woman knew why she was in the Father's presence. Gabriel explained this to her while she was in Nazareth. Would we be wrong to believe that she and the Spirit communicated about sacred things while she was being bodily transported to the presence of the Highest? Further, would it be unreasonable to believe that for a short length of time the veil was taken from her mind and she was able to see the presentation of the Father's plan of salvation before his spirit children, as well as her own calling to be the mortal mother of Jesus Christ? Although not supported by any revealed knowledge, is there any doubt that very rapidly in the Highest's presence his thoughts became her thoughts and his ways became her ways. (Isa. 55:8) Further, even though Mary knew she was espoused to Joseph, she felt no shame, coercion, uneasiness, or hesitancy to become the mother of our Lord. This precious and chosen vessel, willing and without reservation, became the mother of Jesus Christ because of her total love and obedience to the Father and his plan of salvation, which plan called for a Savior and Redeemer. Accordingly, in this most sacred setting, and by their holy union, Mary conceived in her womb God's Son.

We will now present doctrines seldom mentioned, using as much propriety and plainness as possible.

CHAPTER FOURTEEN

RELATIONSHIP OF MARY AND THE FATHER

Regarding gospel mysteries, we shall learn of one that is the least spoken of or understood. Three General Authorities have expressed marvelous and thought-provoking comments regarding the relationship between God the Father and Mary. With the Spirit as our guide, let us discover what has been revealed on this holy and sacred subject.

From Elder Orson Pratt, we read these thought-provoking words:

> "The fleshly[sic] body of Jesus required a Mother as well as a Father. Therefore, the Father and Mother of Jesus, according to the flesh, must have been associated together in the capacity of Husband and Wife; hence the Virgin Mary must have been, for the time being, the *lawful* wife of God the Father: we use the term *lawful* Wife, because it would be blasphemous in the highest degree to say that He overshadowed her or begat the Saviour unlawfully. It would have been unlawful for any *man* to have interfered with Mary, who was already espoused to Joseph; for such a heinous crime would have subjected both the guilty parties to death, according to the law of Moses. But God having created all men and women, had the most perfect right to do with His own creation, according to His holy will and pleasure: He had a lawful

right to overshadow the Virgin Mary in the capacity of a husband, and beget a Son, although she was espoused to another; for the law which He gave to govern men and women was not intended to govern Himself, or to prescribe rules for his own conduct. It was also lawful in Him, after having thus dealt with Mary, to give her to Joseph, her espoused husband. Whether God the Father gave Mary to Joseph for time only, or for time and eternity, we are not informed. Inasmuch as God was the first husband to her, it may be that He only gave her to be the wife of Joseph while in this mortal state, and that He intended after the resurrection to again take her as one of his own wives to raise up immortal spirits in eternity."[54]

In the next monthly publication, Elder Pratt further wrote:

> "We have now clearly shown that God the Father had a plurality of wives, one or more being in eternity, by whom He begat our spirits as well as the spirit of Jesus His First Born, and another being upon the earth by whom He begat the tabernacle of Jesus, as His Only Begotten in this world."[55]

(Elder Orson Pratt was ordained an Apostle, April 26, 1835. He died October 3, 1881.)

In addition to Elder Pratt's comments, President Brigham Young stated:

> "The man Joseph, the husband of Mary, did not, that we know of, have more than one wife, but Mary the wife of Joseph had another husband...That very babe that was cradled in the manger, was begotten, not by Joseph, the

> husband of Mary, but by another being. Do you inquire by whom? He was begotten by God our heavenly [sic] Father."[56]

(Brigham Young became President of the Church on December 27, 1847 and was the Lord's prophet until his death, August 29, 1877.)

Lastly, President Joseph F. Smith declared:

> "Mary was married to Joseph for time. No man could take her for eternity because she belonged to the Father of her divine Son."[57]

(Joseph F. Smith became President of the Church, October 17, 1901 and was the Lord's prophet until his death, November 19, 1918.)

From these enlightening expressions, the reader will have to determine whether "the Father and Mother of Jesus, according to the flesh...[are] associated together in the capacity of Husband and Wife." Whatever their relationship may be, this holy and sacred event transpired exactly as Gabriel had told Mary in Nazareth:

> "The Holy Ghost shall come upon thee, and the power of the Highest shall overshadow thee: therefore also that holy thing [child] which shall be born of thee shall be called the Son of God." (Luke 1:35)

In conclusion, we are not informed of the time Mary was in the presence of God the Father or what was spoken there. What we do know is that when her sacred time with the Highest was over, she was physically carried by the Spirit back to Nazareth.

With this glorious and holy experience behind her, can we begin to comprehend, even in part, what she has seen and experienced? Further, can we fully understand what Mary is feeling both physically and spiritually?

CHAPTER FIFTEEN

MARY WAS WITH CHILD FROM GOD

A DIFFICULT TIME FOR MARY

Now alone, and with awareness that she was espoused to Joseph, yet with child from God the Father, Mary had to come to terms with the people in Nazareth. How will she tell Joseph and many others of what has transpired? What will she do to have them believe her words? After weighing all of her options, she remembered the words of Gabriel regarding her "cousin Elisabeth," who has "conceived a son in her old age" by an act of God. (Luke 1:36) We know from the scriptural record, she will turn to her relative for help and comfort. To better understand Mary's trials and difficulties, we begin by using the words of Elder Bruce R. McConkie:

> "And so we find Mary, about fifteen years of age and inexperienced in meeting the trials of life, under contract to marry one she loved, but with child by the power of the Holy Ghost. We find her in a city of Galilee—rough, rugged, untempered Galilee—where a self-righteous people were quick to condemn, ever ready to punish; where the tongue of gossip would cut her tender feelings to the bone; where she would become a hiss and a byword among her friends and relatives, for she had (as they would view it) committed the sin next only in wickedness to murder. Those among whom she dwelt would no more

> believe her strange tale that an angel had come to her—angels no longer came to mortals, everyone knew that!—or that the Almighty himself was the Father of that which was in her womb; they would no more believe these claims than they would believe the testimony of the fruit of her womb when he testified in their own city that he was the Messiah of whom Isaiah had spoken.
>
> "What course, then, was open to the young virgin? Where could she go for the help and comfort and guidance she so much needed? Had not Gabriel pointed the way? 'Go to thy cousin Elisabeth,' he said. 'She will comfort and sustain thee. She also is with child in a miraculous way—she will understand. She is wise and experienced. She will counsel and help you, and the Lord will give you power to overcome.'"[58]

In time of difficulty and need, every person wants to turn to someone for "help and comfort and guidance." From Luke's record, we know that Mary turned to her relative for this needed assistance. To know more of this Elisabeth, we refer to the scriptural record.

ELISABETH AND ZACHARIAS

From the Apostle Luke, we find out that Elisabeth was a daughter of the priestly order of Aaron. Also, that her husband Zacharias was a priest after the course of Abia. Regarding their individual and collective goodness, we read that "they were both righteous before God, walking in all the commandments and ordinances of the Lord blameless." (Luke 1:5-6)

We further learn that Elisabeth and Zacharias are no longer young, but "both were now well stricken in years." (Luke 1:7) In addition, all of her married life, Elisabeth had been childless. However, by the power of God, and in her advanced age, "Elisabeth conceived" a child. (Luke 1:24)

ELISABETH

Understandably, Elisabeth was experiencing a difficult time in carrying a child at her age. Physically and emotionally, this older women faced challenges and problems that were not as common with younger childbearing women. We also find that because of real concerns over what might be said by friends and relatives, this blessed soul "hid herself" for a period of "five months." (Luke 1:24) In addition, we read that just prior to Mary's visit, Elisabeth came out of seclusion and resumed normal association with people in the community.

How beneficial that Mary, who was young and with child from God, wants to be with her cousin in her time of need. Further, that Elisabeth, who was old and with child from Zacharias, in a miraculous manner from God, needed Mary for special help and care. These different-aged relatives, who loved each other, assisted and comforted each other during a challenging three-month period.

ZACHARIAS

In reference to Zacharias, we read that while this faithful priest was praying while performing his duties in the temple, an angel of the Lord appeared to him. It is the same Gabriel, who will soon appear to Mary, who spoke these surprising words: "Fear not...for thy prayer is heard; and thy wife Elisabeth shall bear thee a son, and thou shalt call his name John." (Luke 1:13) Imagine what this manifestation did to this goodly man. When Gabriel delivered his message, Zacharias spoke to the messenger. Prompted in large measure by age, and in the spirit of doubt and skepticism, he asked the angel, "Whereby shall I know this? for I am an old man, and my wife well stricken in years." (Luke 1:18)

Sometimes signs from heaven come to individuals in ways unexpected; such was the case with Zacharias. Immediately after questioning the angel, this aged priest became deaf and dumb. Zacharias remained this way until eight days after the child was born, when he wrote John's revealed name. (Luke 1:57-64)

During Mary's visit with this elderly couple, Zacharias was unable to verbally communicate with the young maiden or his spouse. However, he was able to communicate by writing, and because Gabriel appeared and spoke with both Zacharias and Mary, each was able to help the other understand spiritual things. Consequently, these three individuals were a great source of help to each other. No wonder Mary was prompted by the angel Gabriel to go to her cousin Elisabeth.

CHAPTER SIXTEEN

MARY TO VISIT ELISABETH

At this difficult time, Mary's emotions were keen. Notwithstanding her feelings, it is safe to assume that Mary was a loving and caring person. Although the scriptures make no mention of them, it is reasonable to believe that Mary's parents were equally caring and loving. We wonder what this young daughter said to her parents regarding her visit to Elisabeth. Because so many personal matters are omitted from the Bible, we are left to draw our own conclusion on the matter. Whatever was said, it is reasonable to believe that the Spirit guided Mary's words, and her parents gave their blessing to go.

We read of another possibility why Mary went to visit her relative:

"Gabriel's announcement about Elisabeth was unspoken counsel to Mary to go and receive comfort and help from her cousin, whom she no doubt loved and revered—the inference is that Mary's mother was dead—and who, being herself with child in a miraculous manner, could speak peace to the young virgin's heart as no other mortal could.[59]

Although not supported by scripture, Elder McConkie's explanation seems plausible and deserves consideration. Perhaps this was one of the reasons why Mary was urged to visit Elisabeth.

If Mary's mother were alive, perhaps she was not able to give her daughter the spiritual understanding and comfort she desperately needed. The only knowledge that we have is that

Mary leaves Nazareth and travels a great distance to be with her cousin, Elisabeth.

DID MARY INFORM JOSEPH?

Turning our attention to Mary's espoused husband, we may wonder what Joseph's knowledge was of Mary's visit with Elisabeth. We read that "Mary arose in those days, and went...with haste...And entered into the house of Zacharias, and saluted Elisabeth." (Luke 1:39-40) Luke's record can leave the impression that Mary tells nothing to Joseph of her visit. Regarding this matter, we again turn to the expressions of Elder McConkie:

> "We may well suppose that Mary told Joseph of her condition; that she then went to Elisabeth; that Joseph struggled with his problem for nearly three months, being fully tested; that Gabriel brought the word; that Joseph sent word to Mary of his conversion; that she returned again in haste and joy; that immediately the second part of the marriage ceremony was performed; and that Joseph, to preserve the virginity of the one who bore God's Child, refrained from sexual association with her until after Jesus came forth as her child."[60]

Again, Elder McConkie's explanation seems plausible. With Mary's loving and caring nature, as well as being righteous before God, it appears out of character for this espoused wife to leave her espoused husband for an extended visit with Elisabeth, saying nothing to him.

RELATIONSHIP OF MARY AND ELISABETH

We are not informed whether Mary was a cousin to Elisabeth on her mother's or father's side of the family. From Edersheim, we read these informative but unsupported words, "...while Mary could also claim kinship with the Priesthood, being, no doubt on her mother's side, a 'blood-relative' of Elisabeth, the Priest-wife of Zacharias."[61]

MARY TRAVELS TO VISIT ELISABETH

Regarding Mary's journey to her cousin, Luke records that she "arose in those days, and went into the hill country with haste, into a city of Juda." (Luke 1:39) From Elder Talmage, we read that "Mary set out with haste from Nazareth for the hill country of Judea, on a journey of about a hundred miles if the traditional account be true that the little town of Juttah was the home of Zacharias."[62]

With another point of view, Elder McConkie writes, that Mary "arose and went in haste to her cousin Elisabeth, a hundred and more miles hence in Hebron of Judea."[63]

Motivated by various reasons, and with deep feelings, Mary journeyed—whether to Juttah or Hebron—a hundred miles or more to be with her beloved cousin. Whether she walked or rode a donkey, we are not informed. Undoubtedly she was escorted by one or more relatives. Certainly, concerns for her personal safety dictated that she not travel alone.

MARY'S TRIALS HAVE BEGUN

Mary's trials in life have just begun. In ten months, and while in the temple in Jerusalem for Jesus' redemption ceremony,[64] she would be told of the greatness of her Son. Further, she would be told of the trials and anguish she would be called to bear because of him; those trials will be like a sword piercing her soul. (Luke 2:25-35) That sword was just beginning to pierce!

Let us discover what happened during the time that Mary was with Elisabeth.

CHAPTER SEVENTEEN

MARY WITH ELISABETH

Both physically and emotionally, this journey was a taxing one for this young maiden. After traveling for days, it was a welcome site to see her relatives' home. Again from Luke, we learn that upon entering "the house of Zacharias," and certainly out of love and respect, Mary "saluted Elisabeth." (Luke 1:40) There was mutual joy and happiness in the meeting between these two cousins. From the scriptural record, we find out "that, when Elisabeth heard the salutation of Mary, the babe leaped in her womb; and Elisabeth was filled with the Holy Ghost." (Luke 1:41)

The Prophet Joseph Smith has revealed that, "The Holy Ghost is a Revelator." Further, "No man can receive the Holy Ghost without receiving revelations."[65] From this revealed truth, we know that Elisabeth was filled with the Holy Ghost, and by revelation this great woman became a living witness that Mary was to be the mother of our Lord. Regarding this special event, Elder Talmage has written these explanatory words:

> "From what of Gabriel's words her husband had communicated, Elisabeth must have known that the approaching birth of her son would soon be followed by that of the Messiah, and that therefore the day for which Israel had waited and prayed through the long dark centuries was about to dawn. When Mary's salutation fell

upon her ears, the Holy Ghost bore witness that the chosen mother of the Lord stood before her in the person of her cousin..."[66]

Continuing again with the scriptural record, we read what Elisabeth said to her beloved relative, "Blessed art thou among women, and blessed is the fruit of thy womb." Out of sweet respect and honor, she then asks Mary this question, "And whence is this to me, that the mother of my Lord should come to me?" Without waiting for a reply, this older cousin gives this surprising information to Mary, "For, lo, as soon as the voice of thy salutation sounded in mine ears, the babe leaped in my womb for joy." From this information, we understand that the unborn John bears witness of this same knowledge. This truly was a miracle of the highest order. This miracle was to two related individuals at once; Elisabeth the mother; and John, the unborn child in her womb. Both of these individuals were witnesses of Mary's divine calling. Then, Elisabeth says to Mary, "And blessed [are thou] that believed [the angel Gabriel]: for there shall be a performance [all shall be fulfilled] of those things which were told [you] from the Lord." (Luke 1:42-45)

Filled with the Holy Ghost herself, "Mary responded with that glorious hymn of praise, since adopted in the musical ritual of churches as the *Magnificat*."[67]

MARY'S MAGNIFICAT

"My soul doth magnify the Lord, and my spirit hath rejoiced in God my Saviour. For he hath regarded the low estate of his handmaiden: for, behold, from henceforth all generations shall call me blessed. For he that is mighty hath done to me great things; and holy is his name. And

> his mercy is on them that fear him from generation to generation. He hath shewed strength with his arm; he hath scattered the proud in the imagination of their hearts. He hath put down the mighty from their seats, and exalted them of low degree. He hath filled the hungry with good things; and the rich he hath sent empty away. He hath holpen [helped] his servant Israel, in remembrance of his mercy; as he spake to our fathers, to Abraham, and to his seed forever."[68] (Luke 1:46-55)

From this glorious information found in the Gospel of Luke, we know that the Holy Ghost bore witness to Elisabeth that Mary was to be the mother of the Messiah. Mary, by the same spirit, spoke great and wonderful words to her cousin. Zacharias, no doubt, also received the same confirmation by the Revelator. Now, if Joseph were to receive this knowledge, Mary would find the peace and comfort that she so earnestly prayed for and desired.

Back in Nazareth, Joseph struggled with his thoughts about Mary's claim that she was with child from God the Father. Let us probe his concerns and actions.

CHAPTER EIGHTEEN

JOSEPH'S DREAM AND ACTION

In the Book of Mormon, Moroni has written these truth-filled words: "I would show unto the world that faith is things which are hoped for and not seen; wherefore, dispute not because ye see not, for ye receive no witness until after the trial of your faith." (Ether 12:6) From this knowledge, we know that Joseph did not receive the witness that Mary was carrying the Father's Son, until after the trial of his faith.

Regarding Mary telling Joseph, we read these moving words:

> "For Joseph it was the beginning of a period of agony and uncertainty. That he wanted to believe Mary, but did not, is shown by his determination 'to put her away privily' with as little embarrassment as possible. He planned to give her a letter of divorce in the presence of two witnesses only, as the law permitted, rather than to make the dissolution of their contract to marry a matter of public knowledge and possible gossip. It must have been at this point that Mary sped hastily to Hebron to find comfort in the arms of Elisabeth."[69]

MARY'S TRIAL WHILE AT ELISABETH'S HOME

Likewise, what of Mary's trial during her three-month time with Elisabeth and Zacharias? Undoubtedly, this was the first time that this young maiden had been away from home, and Joseph, for an extended time. Visualize the number of tears that frequently and easily flowed from her eyes because of her tender and caring emotions. Likewise, picture the sincere prayers of faith she offered for herself, the Holy Child in her womb, for Elisabeth, as well as those for Zacharias. In addition, the prayers for her family members. Most importantly, her greatest desire was for Joseph to know that she was with child from God the Father. She needed a husband to help her with this tremendous responsibility. If she went back to Nazareth unmarried and expecting a child, what would the community do to her? After all of the wonderful and sacred things she had seen and experienced, why was Joseph so unwilling to believe her words? We can, in part, understand the challenges and trials she was experiencing.

During this difficult time for Mary and Joseph, it is reasonable to believe that both Elisabeth and Zacharias offered earnest prayers of faith for and in behalf of this couple.

JOSEPH, IN NAZARETH

In Nazareth, Joseph struggled with his thoughts and feelings. He pondered and prayed frequently. This goodly man sincerely wanted to know if his espoused wife was with child from God or by another man. Joseph truly loved his beloved Mary with all of his heart. He also knew of her goodness and quality. Further, he also knew that she had never lied to him. Yet, could she really be with child by the Highest? His doubts and frustrations were real. We do not know exactly how long Joseph struggled with his concerns. All that we know is that after his trial was over, he finally received an answer.

JOSEPH'S DREAM

The scriptural record informs us that during the night, "...the angel of the Lord appeared unto him in a dream." (Matt. 1:20) This angel was the same Gabriel who appeared to both Zacharias and Mary. This heavenly messenger instructed this concerned man, "Joseph, thou son of David, fear not to take unto thee Mary thy [espoused] wife: for that which is conceived in her is [by the power] of the Holy Ghost." The angel further tells him, "And she shall bring forth a son, and thou shalt call his name JESUS: for he shall save his people from their sins." (Matt. 1:20-21)

Because of his dream-vision, Joseph no longer doubted that his beloved Mary was indeed with child from God. Because of this special manifestation, we can sense the peace he was finally feeling, mixed with an urgent desire to let Mary know of his dream.

DREAMS AND VISIONS

A person may wonder why he received his vision at night while asleep, instead of during the daytime, as did Zacharias and Mary. To help answer this, we read in the Book of Mormon about Lehi. He reveals this meaningful doctrine, "Behold, I have dreamed a dream; or, in other words, I have seen a vision." (1 Ne. 8:2) From this scripture, we discover that dreams and visions are closely related. Based on this information, we know that Gabriel delivered his message to this espoused husband in like manner as he did with Zacharias and

Mary. Perhaps one reason Joseph received his vision in a dream was that he was physically and mentally relaxed and less perplexed about Mary's condition; thereby, he was more receptive to receive spiritual knowledge.

Regarding Joseph's dream, we turn to the expressions of Edersheim:

> "The fact that such an announcement came to him in a dream, would dispose Joseph all the more readily to receive it. 'A good dream' was...popularly regarded as marks of God's favour [sic]...Thus Divinely set at rest, Joseph could no longer hesitate. The highest duty towards the Virgin-Mother and the unborn Jesus demanded an immediate marriage, which would afford not only outward, but moral protection to both."[70]

In brief yet profound words, Matthew writes, "Then Joseph being raised from sleep did as the angel of the Lord had bidden him, and took unto him his wife." (Matt. 1:24) It is no surprise that this dream-vision woke Joseph from his sleep. Immediately upon waking, it is easy to sense the urgency this blessed man felt to let his espoused wife to know of his vision. We are not informed how Joseph contacted Mary with the good news or how many days it took his message to go from Nazareth to Zacharias' home. No doubt it was several long and anxious days. All that we know is that as quickly as he could, this espoused husband was able to communicate to his espoused wife of his visit from Gabriel, and his sincere desire to complete the second part of their marriage ceremony.

CHAPTER NINETEEN

MARRIAGE OF MARY AND JOSEPH

It is beyond question that Mary was overjoyed and grateful for Joseph's message. All that is written—perhaps all that was needed to be written—is this short and informative statement: "And Mary...returned to her own house." (Luke 1:56) Again, we are not informed how she traveled to Nazareth or with whom or how many days it took. All that we know is that the long journey to her home was accomplished.

After their long and trying absence, picture the warm and joyous meeting between Mary and Joseph; the wholesome and affectionate embraces that were given; and the tender and loving words that were exchanged between them. Mary was finally able to tell Joseph of spiritual things that never before could be spoken. This meeting was a special time for this unique couple.

We are not informed how soon Mary and Joseph completed the second part of the marriage ceremony. It no doubt was within a short time after Mary returned home. It is reasonable to believe that this second ceremony was similar to most marriages that were performed in their day. We again turn to our Jewish scholar for information:

A JEWISH WEDDING

"On the evening of the actual marriage...the bride was led from her paternal home to that of her husband.

> First came the merry sounds of music; then they who distributed among the people wine and oil, and nuts among the children; next the bride, covered with the bridal veil, her long hair flowing, surrounded by her companions, and led by 'the friends of the bridegroom,' and 'the children of the bride-chamber.' All around were in festive array; some carried torches, or lamps on poles; those nearest had myrtle-branches and chaplets of flowers. Everyone rose to salute the procession, or join it; and it was deemed almost a religious duty to break into praise of the beauty, the modesty, or the virtues of the bride. Arrived at her new home, she was led to her husband. Some such formula as 'Take her according to the Law of Moses and of Israel,' would be spoken, and bride and bridegroom crowned with garlands. Then a formal legal instrument, called the Kethubah, was signed, which set forth that the bridegroom undertook to work for her, to honour, [sic] keep, and care for her, as is the manner of the men of Israel...Then, after the prescribed washing of hands and benediction, the marriage-supper began—the cup being filled, and the solemn prayer of bridal benediction spoken over it. And so the feast lasted—it might be more than one day—while each sought to contribute, sometimes coarsely, sometimes wisely, to the general enjoyment, till at last 'the friends of the bridegroom' led the bridal pair to the Cheder and the Chuppah, or the bridal chamber and bed..."[71]

Using as much propriety as possible, we know that when their friends "led the bridal pair to the...bridal chamber and bed" that Joseph and Mary did not consummate their marriage until after she gave birth to the Christ Child. We know this to be so, for Matthew has written: "And [Joseph] knew her not till she had brought forth her firstborn son: and he called his name JESUS." (Matt. 1:25)

AFTER MARY AND JOSEPH WERE MARRIED

With their wedding completed by the second ceremony, Mary was now safe and secure from gossip and possible death. Joseph would provide and take care of his bride and her unborn child. Mary was carrying in her womb a God. However, to the community, this child will only be known as the "carpenter's son." (Matt. 13:55) Mary and Joseph were happy, and awaited the blessed day that Jesus will be born. For approximately six months, this special couple prepared their home, and their lives, to be worthy of the birth of the Savior of the world.

MARY AND JOSEPH PREPARED FOR JESUS' BIRTH

It is difficult for us to fully understand what Mary felt daily carrying in her womb the Promised Messiah. However, we can picture how kind and respectful Joseph was to the mother of our Lord and likewise, the kindness and love that Mary gave Joseph. In order to preserve the virgin birth of the Father's Son, Joseph is admirably lauded for his control and composure to not know his wife until after Jesus was born. Based on these qualities, we can, in part, begin to appreciate the quality and goodness of this special couple. With this information, we can better understand why Christ was to be born into the family of Mary and Joseph.

The time was fast approaching for the birth of the greatest person ever born. What events surrounded our Lord's birth? What transpired in the lives of Mary and Joseph following the birth of the Christ Child? Let us learn of these glorious happenings.

CHAPTER TWENTY

JOURNEY TO BETHLEHEM

Nearly six months passed since Mary and Joseph were formally married by the second ceremony. They were adjusting to married life, as well as the realization that they were the designated guardians of the Son of God. During this time, Mary experienced all of the physical and emotional changes associated with being an expectant mother. Being big with child, in the final month, we can understand the difficulty she had in sitting, sleeping, and the day-to-day activities of being a wife and a homemaker.

Knowing his wife's condition, Joseph did all that he could to help Mary during this adjustment time. Further, Joseph had tremendous control and respect toward Mary not to physically know her. (Matt. 1:25)

As Mary and Joseph were going through a new dimension in their lives, it is easy to picture the love and harmony that existed in their humble home and, likewise, to hear the earnest prayers of faith which were offered together, and privately, to God the Father, to prepare them to raise his Beloved Son.

...TO BE TAXED

Within a short time prior to Mary giving birth, "there went out a decree from Caesar Augustus, that all the world should be taxed... And all went to be taxed, every one into his own city." (Luke 2:1-3) Regarding this taxing, we turn to Elder Talmage for clarification:

> "At that time a decree went out from Rome ordering a taxing of the people in all kingdoms and provinces tributary to the empire...The taxing herein referred to may properly be understood as an enrolment [sic], or a registration, whereby a census of Roman subjects would be secured, upon which as a basis the taxation of the different peoples would be determined."

Then, as it pertains to this blessed husband and wife, Elder Talmage gives this insightful information:

> "Had the census been taken by the usual Roman method, each person would have been enrolled at the town of his residence; but the Jewish custom, for which the Roman law had respect, necessitated registration at the cities or towns claimed by the respective families as their ancestral homes...certain it is that Joseph and Mary went to Bethlehem, the city of David, to be inscribed under the imperial decree."[72]

There are two apparent reasons why Joseph and Mary went to Bethlehem: (1)The ruler Caesar had spoken. Even the Jewish people had to comply with Roman law. Being law-abiding citizens, Joseph and his wife left Nazareth and traveled to their mutual ancestral town. (2)This "imperial decree" was only a means of fulfilling prophecy. Prophets of old revealed that the City of David was the designated place where our Lord will be born. In Micah 5:2, we read: "But thou, Bethlehem Ephratah, though thou be little among the thousands of Judah, yet out of thee shall he come forth unto me that is to be ruler in

Israel; whose goings forth have been from old, from everlasting." Both Mary and Joseph knew of these prophecies. Therefore, by reasons of the taxation decree and the prophecies that must be fulfilled, this special couple left their home and journeyed to the designated town where the "ruler in Israel" was to be born.

By reason of the prophecies, some may wonder why Joseph and Mary did not live in Bethlehem instead of Nazareth. It seems logical that since they were both born in Nazareth, and their parental families lived there, Mary and Joseph desired to live in this town. In addition, we read from the scriptural record, "that it might be fulfilled which was spoken by the prophets, He shall be called a Nazarene." (Matt. 2:23) Accordingly, this couple resided in Nazareth instead of their ancestral town.

Because of the taxation decree, a great number of people left Nazareth and went to their various ancestral towns. In Bethlehem, there were limited number of rooms to stay in. Mary was due to give birth any day. We are left to wonder why Joseph and Mary did not leave earlier than they did. It is apparent that divine providence caused them a late start in order that Jesus would be born in "the most humble circumstances."73

Further, "...they were traversing a journey of eighty miles to the village which had been the home of their great ancestor..."74

There are so many personal matters omitted from the scriptures that we are not informed if Mary and Joseph walked or rode a donkey to Bethlehem, or, additionally, if they traveled alone or with relatives and friends. Whatever the case, we know that Mary was big with child, and this journey was long and challenging.

NO ROOM IN THE INN

Using again the expressions of Farrar, we read:

> "Traveling in the East is a very slow and leisurely affair...But the heavy languor, [lacking physical or mental energy] or even the commencing pangs of travail, must necessarily have retarded the progress of the maiden-mother. Others who were traveling on the same errand would easily have passed them on the road, and when...they arrived at the [manger, which Farrar calls by the following name:] khan...every leewan [room] was occupied. The enrollment had drawn so many strangers to the little town that 'there was no room for them in the inn.' (Luke 2:7)"[75]

After this tiring journey, we can understand the fatigue and anxiety which Mary and Joseph both felt upon finding no suitable lodging. We know that this blessed couple was finally able to find lodging and rest, and to lay the newborn child in a place called a "manger." (Luke 2:7)

The greatest person on this earth was to be born—our Lord and Savior, Jesus Christ. Let us read what is revealed on this holy subject.

CHAPTER TWENTY-ONE

JESUS' BIRTH

As Farrar has explained, this manger was actually called a *kahn*. In describing one, we learn that everything that took place in them was visible to every person. The traveler brought his own food, attended his own animals, and drew his own water. He paid a small fee for the advantage of the shelter. Further, if the person seeking a place to stay arrived late, and all of the rooms were full, he and his family would have to stay in the courtyard below and find little cleanliness and decency. He would share this area with horses, mules, and camels. The closeness of the quarters and the unpleasant smells would ever be present in this stable area. (*See The Life of Christ*, pp. 2-3)

Then Farrar informs us that kahns were located in the "innumerable caves which abound in the limestone rocks of its central hills."[76]

Because there was no room in the inn, Mary and Joseph were staying in a manger in Bethlehem. In some degree, we can understand the mixed feelings and emotions that this couple was experiencing. Any time now, Mary would give birth to a baby, and this Holy Child was the long awaited Promised Messiah, the "Deliverer" of Israel. Sense the joyous feelings surrounding this holy event. Yet, Mary and Joseph were in a stable, mingled with animals and people, with all of the attendant noises and smells. This, too, aroused another set of feelings.

The time for Jesus to be born arrived. Mary suddenly felt

sharp, strong, and regular labor pains. Joseph had anxious concerns and feelings for his wife. We may wonder, when Mary cried out in pain, did other women in the manger come to her aid or was Joseph the only assistant?

WHEN OUR SAVIOR WAS BORN

There are a number of unanswered questions surrounding the birth of our Lord. One of these is the month, day, and year that this blessed event transpired. There are a variety of scholarly opinions, both in and out of the Church, on this subject. In a book that is approved by the Church, *Jesus the Christ*, Elder James E. Talmage has written these declarative words: "We believe that Jesus Christ was born in Bethlehem of Judea, April 6, B.C. 1." (p. 104) In addition, modern apostles and prophets have stated that our Lord was born on the sixth day of April. (*See* note 1 at the end of this chapter.)

According to the world, all that is known about the birth of our Lord is what the Apostle Luke has written: "And so it was, that, while they were there, the days were accomplished that she should be delivered. And she brought forth her first-born son, and wrapped him in swaddling clothes, and laid him in a manger; because there was no room for them in the inn." (Luke 2:6-7)

With Jesus just minutes old, picture this special mother holding this holy boy with tender and reverent affection. Visualize the respect and love Joseph gave to his wife and the Christ Child. After giving birth to a planned-for child, a mother's love is strong and true; there is an immediate bonding. Comprehend the love Mary had for Jesus. Not only was this her child, but he was also her Savior and Redeemer!

A God was born in mortality. From his mother, he inherited all of the powers associated with mortality; from his Father he inherited all of the powers of immortality. In approximately thirty-three years, our Lord would work out the infinite and eternal atonement. This holy act would be accomplished with the unique body he inherited from his parents. Heavenly manifestations proceeded and attended his birth. In addition to heavenly manifestations that were seen in Palestine, others were witnessed in the Americas. (3 Ne. 1:4-5; 15; 21; Hel. 14:3-6) Let us read of these manifestations in Palestine.

NOTES

1. The year of our Lord's birth has been calculated from B.C. 1 to B.C. 7. Further, the month and day has been declared to be sometime between December 25 and April 6. For a more thorough study on this subject, this reader is referred to two works: (1)James E. Talmage, *Jesus the Christ*. 1962. pp. 102-104; 109; (2)Bruce R. McConkie, *The Mortal Messiah: From Bethlehem to Calvary*. Book 1 (Salt Lake City: Deseret Book, 1979), note 2, pp. 349-350.

Gordon B. Hinckley, who was then a member of the Council of the Twelve Apostles, President Spencer W. Kimball and President Harold B. Lee all state that it was the sixth of April that Jesus Christ was born. The reader is referred to an address, February 3, 1980, Joseph Smith Memorial Lecture, p. 2; Conference Report, April 5, 1974, page 4; Conference Report, April 4, 1975, pp. 3-4; Conference Report, April 6, 1973, p.4. A counselor in the First Presidency, Charles W. Nibley, also states that it was the sixth of April when Christ was born—*See* Conference Report, April 6, 1930, pp. 26-27.

CHAPTER TWENTY-TWO

MANIFESTATIONS FROM HEAVEN

In the Old World, by or in the hills surrounding Bethlehem, we learn of a heavenly manifestation having taken place. From Elder Talmage, we read these insightful words:

> "It is quite in line with what is known of the town and its environs to find at the season of Messiah's birth, which was in the springtime of the year, that flocks were in the field both night and day under the watchful care of their keepers. Unto certain of these humble shepherds came the first proclamation that the Savior had been born. Thus runs the simple record: 'And there were in the same country shepherds abiding in the field, keeping watch over their flock by night. And, lo, the angel of the Lord came upon them [It is reasonable to believe that it is the same Gabriel who appeared to Zacharias, Mary, and Joseph] and the glory of the Lord shone round about them: and they were sore afraid. And the angel said unto them, Fear not: for, behold, I bring you good tidings of great joy, which shall be to all people. For unto you is born this day in the city of David a Saviour, which is Christ the Lord. And this shall be a sign unto you: Ye shall find the babe wrapped in swaddling clothes, lying in a manger." (Luke 2: 8-12)[77]

Imagine what these righteous shepherds must have felt upon seeing this angelic appearance and hearing his message. In the first appearance, there was only one heavenly messenger; then, as the record reads: "And suddenly there was with the angel a multitude of the heavenly host praising God, and saying, Glory to God in the highest, and on earth peace, good will toward men." (Luke 2:13-14) Truly this was a marvelous manifestation from heaven!

Again, we read the words of Elder Talmage:

> "The trustful and unsophisticated keepers of sheep had not asked for sign or confirmation...nevertheless the angel had given them what he called a sign, to guide them in their search. They waited not, but went in haste, for in their hearts they believed, yea, more than believed, they knew, and this was the tenor of their resolve: 'Let us now go even unto Bethlehem, and see this thing which is come to pass, which the Lord hath made known unto us.' (Luke 2:15) They found the Babe in the manger, with the mother and Joseph near by...[sic]"[78]

THE SHEPHERDS VISITED THE CHRIST CHILD

Picture these blessed shepherds (how many we are not informed) entering the manger and respectfully and reverently approaching Mary and her child. Then, see each kneel and worship the baby Lord. Further, listen to one or all in turn telling of the angel's message and the inspiring music that was sung by the heavenly host. Imagine how this message touched Mary's and Joseph's hearts. When the shepherds left, the record states: "they made known abroad the saying which was told them concerning this child. And all they that heard it wondered at those things...." (Luke 2:17-18)

There is a time and a place for everything. In a future day, Mary would become one of her Son's most faithful followers, and she would testify of Jesus' divinity. For now, however, on this special day, this was her newborn child. Accordingly, what Luke has written was appropriate for the occasion: "But Mary kept all these things, and pondered them in her heart." (Luke 2:19)

THE STAY IN THE MANGER

Some individuals may wonder how long this special family resided in the manger. To answer, we turn to the thoughts and expressions of Farrar:

> "How long the Virgin Mother and her holy Child stayed in this cave, or cattle-inclosure[sic], we cannot tell, but probably it was not for long... It is probable that the crowd in the kahn would not be permanent, and common humanity would have dictated an early removal of the mother and her child to some more appropriate resting-place."79

It is reasonable to believe that shortly following their individual taxation enrollment, masses of Jews who came to Bethlehem left and returned to their respective homes. Thereby, this exodus afforded opportunity for Joseph's family to find lodging more fitting than in the stable. Sense the relief and thankfulness of Mary and Joseph for this relocation move.

After Jesus was born, he and his mother obeyed Jewish law regarding his birth. Let us learn of this requirement.

CHAPTER TWENTY-THREE

MARY AND JESUS OBEYED JEWISH LAW

To be in compliance with the Law of Moses, we discover that this unique family resided in Bethlehem for at least forty days. To help us understand about the "law," we turn to Elder Talmage for understanding:

> "The Child was born a Jew; the mother was a Jewess, and the reputed and legal father, Joseph, was a Jew...The requirements of the law were carried out with exactitude in all matters pertaining to the Child. When eight days old He was circumcised, as was required of every male born in Israel; and at the same time He received as an earthly bestowal the name that had been prescribed at the annunciation. He was called Jesus, which, being interpreted, is Savior; the name was rightfully His for He came to save the people from their sins."[80]

We are not informed of who was allowed to perform the required circumcision. Evidently, the rite was performed by an authorized individual who verified that the law was obeyed.

As it relates to Jesus' mother, Elder Talmage gives this explanation:

> "Part of the law given through Moses to the

Israelites in the wilderness and continued in force down through the centuries, related to the procedure prescribed for women after childbirth. In compliance therewith, Mary remained in retirement forty days following the birth of her Son; then she and her husband brought the Boy for presentation before the Lord as prescribed for the male firstborn of every family."[81]

Regarding Mary and her son, we read these words:

> "Jesus was born within five or six miles from Jerusalem; He was accordingly taken to the temple for the ceremonial of redemption from the requirement applying to the firstborn of all Israelites except Levites. It will be remembered that the children of Israel had been delivered from the bondage of Egypt with the accompaniment of signs and wonders. Because of Pharaoh's repeated refusals to let the people go, plagues had been brought upon the Egyptians, one of which was the death of the firstborn throughout the land, excepting only the people of Israel. In remembrance of this manifestation of power, the Israelites were required to dedicate their firstborn sons to the service of the sanctuary. Subsequently the Lord directed that all males belonging to tribe of Levi should be devoted to this special labor instead of the firstborn in every tribe; nevertheless the eldest son was still claimed as particularly the Lord's own, and had to be formally exempted from the earlier requirement of service by paying of a ransom."[82]

Regarding the "ransom" amount paid to redeem the first-born son, Edersheim has written that this cost was "the price of five shekels."[83]

Continuing again with the words of Elder Talmage, we

read:

> "In connection with the ceremony of purification, every mother was required to furnish a yearling lamb for a burnt offering, and a young pigeon or dove for a sin offering; but in the case of any woman who was unable to provide a lamb, a pair of doves or pigeons might be offered. We learn of the humble circumstances of Joseph and Mary from the fact that they brought the less costly offering, two doves or pigeons, instead of one bird and a lamb."[84]

With all of the requirements met, Mary, her child, and Joseph were able to leave the temple and prepare to travel to Nazareth. To this couple's surprise, at that time two unrelated people testified of Jesus' divinity. Luke reports that the first was a man by the name of Simeon, and the other was a woman by the name of Anna. Let us listen to what was spoken of Mary's divine Son.

CHAPTER TWENTY-FOUR

PRAISING WORDS FOR MARY'S SON

SIMEON AND ANNA

Simeon was an elderly man who was righteous. Prior to entering the temple this day, the Holy Ghost "revealed unto him...that he should not see death, before he had seen the Lord's Christ." (Luke 2:26)

Visualize Simeon slowly approaching the Holy Family and gesturing to Mary that he be allowed to take the baby Jesus from her arms? See her willingly consent to this individual's request. For as Luke has written:

> "Then took he him up in his arms, and blessed God, and said,
>
> "Lord, now lettest thou thy servant depart in peace, according to thy word:
>
> "For mine eyes have seen thy salvation,
>
> "Which thou has prepared before the face of all people;
>
> "A light to lighten the Gentiles, and the glory of thy people Israel." (Luke 2:28-32)

This is the first recorded New Testament testimony that salvation comes by and through our Savior. Further, that Christ will bring light and knowledge to the Gentiles, as well as glorious truths to Israel's people.

Next Simeon blessed this righteous couple and said to Mary:

> "...Behold, this child is set for the fall and rising again of many in Israel; and for a sign which shall be spoken against;
>
> "(Yea, a sword shall pierce through thy own soul also,) that the thoughts of many hearts may be revealed." (Luke 2:34-35)

This inspired man revealed that the words of our Lord will cause men and women to fall or rise as they either believe or disbelieve his words; that he will be a sign or symbol of righteousness that many will speak out against; and that Mary will experience pain and sorrow because of how people will mock and eventually hang her beloved child on the cross. Lastly, because of this child's divinity, he will be able to reveal people's true thoughts and motives.

As soon as Simeon returned the infant to his mother's arms, we are informed that a woman named Anna, who was of great age and spirituality, approached near and spoke similar words of recognition and praise. For as the scriptural record briefly states, "And she coming in that instant gave thanks likewise unto the Lord, and spake of him to all them that looked for redemption in Jerusalem." (Luke 2:38)

From what they have just heard from Simeon and Anna, the record states, "And Joseph and his mother marvelled at those things which were spoken of him." (Luke 2:33) Even though this couple saw and heard Gabriel, and they knew that Jesus was the Christ; yet, at this particular moment they have not fully comprehended "the majesty of Him who had come to them through so miraculous a conception and so marvelous a birth."[85]

In a short time, two spiritually attuned people have borne witness of the divinity of our Lord. Regarding testimony, we read: "In the mouth of two or three witnesses shall every word be established." (2 Cor. 13:1) Since the birth of Jesus, the shepherds have spoken that they have seen the Christ; so also has Simeon and Anna. As time goes on, many others will bear similar testimony.

There are a total of four recorded events of Jesus' infancy. Mary was present at each of them. Let us learn what they are.

CHAPTER TWENTY-FIVE

THE INFANCY OF MARY'S SON

DIFFERENCES IN LUKE'S AND MATTHEW'S GOSPEL

Regarding our Lord's infancy, we read these words of Farrar:

> "Four other events only of our Lord's infancy are narrated by the Gospels—namely, the Circumcision, the Presentation in the Temple, the Visit of the Magi and the Flight into Egypt. Of these the first two occur only in St. Luke, the last two only in St. Matthew. Yet no single particular can be pointed out in which the two narratives are necessarily contradictory...those narratives may fairly be regarded as supplementing each other...Anecdotes of infancy, incidents of childhood, indications of future greatness in boyish years are a very rare phenomenon in ancient literature. It is only since the dawn of Christianity that childhood has been surrounded by a halo of romance."[86]

LUKE'S GOSPEL

As has been written, Luke only records the incidents regarding the "Circumcision" and the "Presentation in the Temple." From his Gospel, we are informed that following their experiences in the temple, Mary, Joseph, and Jesus "returned into Galilee, to their own city Nazareth." (Luke 2:39)

MATTHEW'S GOSPEL

In Matthew's Gospel, however, it states that "...Jesus was born in Bethlehem of Judaea in the days of Herod the king, behold, there came wise men from the east to Jerusalem." (Matt. 2:1) Later, he informs us: "And when they were come into the house, they saw the young child with Mary his mother, and fell down, and worshipped him: and when they had opened their treasures, they presented unto him gifts; gold, and frankincense, and myrrh." (Matt. 2:11. Italics added)

COMBINING THE GOSPELS

Combining the two records, Elder McConkie explains:

> "No reason is given why Joseph took his family the 180 miles or so—on foot, by donkey, or however—from Bethlehem to Nazareth and back. Perhaps they had decided to live in the land of their ancestors, near the sacred events that already had become so much a part of their very being. Their brief return visit in Nazareth may have been to close the carpentry shop and to take leave of friends and loved ones. We have already noted the view that Zacharias was slain by Herod's order when he refused to reveal the hiding place of the child John. Since we have no reason to believe that Herod's assassins were slaying children as far away as Hebron, this gives rise to the thought that Zacharias and Elisabeth may also have chosen Bethlehem for their home. Perhaps Mary and Elisabeth desired to be near each other. It does appear that

when the Holy Family returned from Egypt, Joseph intended to settle again in Bethlehem, but was sent instead by angelic decree to Nazareth."[87]

THE WISE MEN

From Matthew, we discover that Herod sent "wise men" to Bethlehem to find the Messiah; guided by the star as well as by the Spirit, these attuned men found the child. (Matt. 2:1-12) In reference to their visit, we turn to Dr. Edersheim for comment:

> "It could not be difficult to learn in Bethlehem, where the Infant...might be found. It appears that the temporary shelter of the 'stable' had been exchanged by the Holy Family for a more permanent abode of a 'house'; and there the Magi found the Infant-Saviour with His Mother. With exquisite tact and reverence the narrative attempts not the faintest description of the scene."[88]

We are not informed whether Joseph was present on this occasion, but it seems reasonable to believe that he was. We see these wise men—how many there were, we are not informed—approaching the house and with respect asking permission to enter and see the Savior. We know nothing of what was spoken or how long they stayed. All that is written is that they "fell down, and worshipped" our Lord, and presented him expensive gifts. (Matt. 2:11)

Matthew informs us that "when they were departed, behold, the angel of the Lord appeareth to Joseph in a dream, saying, Arise, and take the young child and his mother, and flee into Egypt, and be thou there until I bring thee word: for Herod will seek the young child to destroy him." (Matt. 2:13) Let us learn what happens because of Joseph's dream.

CHAPTER TWENTY-SIX

OUT OF EGYPT

Once again, Joseph received a vision in a dream. As the head of his household, and being attuned to the Spirit, Joseph was able to receive guidance from on high. Knowing that her husband was divinely instructed, Mary prepared herself and Jesus for the journey. While it was dark outside, they gathered their belongings and provisions and closed up the house. We read that Joseph, now readied, "took the young child and his mother by night, and departed into Egypt." (Matt. 2:14) In this country, traveling in the dark was a challenging affair, especially with a young child. Truly this was an obedient couple, who were willing to serve God no matter what the sacrifice or cost. Regarding their stay in Egypt, we turn to Farrar for information:

> "Egypt has, in all ages, been the natural place of refuge for all who were driven from Palestine by distress, persecution or discontent. Rhinokolura, the river of Egypt...might have been reached by the fugitives in three days; and once upon the further bank, they were beyond the reach of Herod's jurisdiction.
>
> "Of the flight, and its duration, Scripture gives us no further particulars; telling us only that the Holy Family fled by night from Bethlehem, and returned when Joseph had again been assured by a dream that it would be safe to take back the Saviour to the land of His nativity."[89]

Elder Talmage gives us this insight:

> "Joseph, Mary, and her Son remained in Egypt until after the death of Herod the Great, which event was made known by another angelic visitation. Their stay in the foreign land was probably brief, for Herod did not long survive the babes he had slain in Bethlehem. In the return of the family from Egypt the evangelist finds a fulfilment of Hosea's prophetic vision of what should be: 'Out of Egypt have I called my son.' (Hos. 11:1)
>
> "It appears to have been Joseph's intention to make a home for the family in Judea, possibly at Bethlehem—the city of his ancestors and a place now even more endeared to him as the birthplace of Mary's Child—but, learning on the way that Herod's son Archelaus ruled in the place of his wicked father, Joseph modified his purpose; and, 'being warned of God in a dream, he turned aside into the parts of Galilee: and he came and dwelt in a city called Nazareth: that it might be fulfilled which was spoken by the prophets, He shall be called a Nazarene.' [(Luke 2:19-23)]"[90]

From this time until Jesus was presented in the temple, at age twelve, we know nothing of the home life of Mary, Joseph, and Jesus. Regarding this timeframe, Elder Talmage wrote these fitting words:

> "The silence with which the early period of the life of Jesus [also that same time regarding Mary and Joseph] is treated by the inspired historians is impressive; while the fanciful accounts written in later years by unauthorized hands are full of fictitious detail, much of which is positively revolting in its puerile inconsistency. None but

> Joseph, Mary, and the other members of the immediate family or close associates of the household could have furnished the facts of daily life in the humble home at Nazareth; and from these qualified informants Matthew and Luke probably derived the knowledge of which they wrote... Read thoughtfully the attested truth concerning the childhood of the Christ: 'And the child grew, and waxed strong in spirit, filled with wisdom: and the grace of God was upon him.' [(Luke 2:40)]"[91]

From the scriptures and inspired writers, we can more fully understand that Mary's life was full of challenge and wonderment. As her child grew older, Mary experienced greater amazement and trial. Let us explore these rewarding but challenging times.

CHAPTER TWENTY-SEVEN

MARY'S SON INCREASED IN WISDOM AND STATURE

In Nazareth, Mary watched Jesus grow and mature both physically and spiritually. We may safely assume that her divine son experienced mortality as all individuals do. He cut teeth, shed tears, laughed, and spoke his first words. He learned to walk and run. Jesus also became hungry and thirsty. If he was to truly experience mortality, it is reasonable to believe he had his share of falls, cuts, bruises, and childhood diseases. Further, our Lord played with his half-brothers and sisters as well as children in the neighborhood. In addition, he learned to share and give. Likewise, he learned manners and a variety of social skills. From study and exercise, our Lord developed his mind and muscles. He observed and learned much from nature, people, and the Spirit. Both physically and spiritually, Jesus increased in wisdom and stature. (Luke 2:52)

As was the custom in that day, Jesus was first taught in the home by his mother; then by his stepfather, Joseph. He observed and participated in daily family prayers. He also learned the duties and observances of the law of Moses, and further, the provisions and meanings of the Mezuzah, Torah, and Shema.[92] He attended the synagogue and heard the prayers and teachings given therein. At five or six years of age, Jesus attended school and continued his formal education until he became a son of the law, which took place at twelve years of age. This most gifted child participated in Jewish feasts and celebrations. In addition, he became acquainted with the prophets and their teachings; especially those who spoke of him.

Because of his pre-eminent position in the premortal life, he brought into this world the gifts and talents he so richly earned there. It needs to be emphasized that by being sinless, Jesus was entitled to the constant companionship of the Holy Ghost. Accordingly, at a very early age, this Divine Son was in tune with his Father in Heaven, and his temporal and spiritual knowledge came rapidly and abundantly, far exceeding those of his fellow mortals. By being mortal, Jesus experienced passions and desires, the same as other men did. However, by reason of his nature and calling, he perfectly controlled his thoughts and actions.

Are we amiss to believe that throughout his younger years that this most dutiful mother told Jesus of his Father in Heaven, and of the sacred and marvelous experiences that transpired? Are we wrong to believe that Joseph also informed him of spiritual happenings, or further, that during these sacred conversations, the Spirit strongly bore record of the truthfulness of the words spoken? Truly there was love and admiration between Jesus, Mary, and Joseph.

MARY'S LIFE WITH JESUS

It is natural to wonder what this special family's life was like from the time they arrived back in Nazareth until at the Passover feast, when our Lord was age twelve. Because Jesus was the Messiah and constantly had the Holy Ghost with him, his spiritual and temporal knowledge came rapidly and abundantly. Due to his rapid learning, it is safe to assume that Mary and Joseph experienced his development with perplexity and amazement. From the record, we learn that Mary, Joseph, and other individuals, from time to time, "marvelled at those things which were spoken of him." In addition, they were "astonished at his understanding and answers," further, "they were amazed." It is also written that on a certain occasion, "they understood not the saying which he spake unto them." (*See* Luke 2:33; 47; 48; 50)

Over this twelve-year span, we can safely assume that Mary knew of many marvelous and miraculous things that Jesus said and did. However, because she was human, and experienced the day-to-day activities of being a wife and mother, it is understandable that Mary occasionally marveled at Jesus' wisdom. Therefore, we read that she was frequently "astonished at his understanding and answers." (Luke 2:47)

As with all good and observant mothers, Mary knew of her divine son's mannerisms and ways. She was aware of his accelerated knowledge and godly attributes. Though Jesus was respectful and obedient, imagine the concerns and worries Mary often experienced because of this unique Son. With his rapid development, how could she properly instruct and teach a God? How could she fully know of his needs and provide them for him? With other children in the home, how was she able to maintain her control and composure in order to keep the Spirit there? Because he was the Christ, how could she keep from favoring him above her other children? Mary knew of her mortal faults and shortcomings; she also knew that Jesus knew them. Due to these real concerns, it is without question that Mary offered fervent prayers to the Father asking for his help and guidance.

We now turn our attention to Jesus' half-brothers and sisters and read what has been revealed on this subject.

CHAPTER TWENTY-EIGHT

MARY AND JOSEPH'S CHILDREN

In Jesus' day, Jewish parents desired to have children, and considered it a blessing to have such. Birth control was not practiced nor was the size of the family limited, as is the case in our modern day. From Psalms, we read these informative words:

> "Lo, children are an heritage of the Lord: and the fruit of the womb is his reward. As arrows are in the hand of a mighty man; so are children of the youth. Happy is the man that hath his quiver full of them: they shall not be ashamed...." (Psalm 127:3-5)

Based upon this information, we can accurately state that Mary and Joseph wanted additional children. From Matthew's Gospel, we know that this husband and wife had at least four sons and more than one daughter. We read that when our Savior's formal ministry began, the people in Nazareth "were astonished, and said, Whence hath this man this wisdom, and these mighty works? Is not this the carpenter's son? Is not his mother called Mary? and his brethren, James, and Joses, and Simon, and Judas? And his sisters, are they not all with us? Whence then hath this man all these things?" (Matt. 13:54-56)

Mark's Gospel also names the Lord's half-brothers, with one exception. He writes the name of Juda instead of Judas. (6:3) In the epistle of Jude, this half-brother of Jesus refers to himself as "Jude, the servant of Jesus Christ, and brother of James...." (Jude 1:1) Although there appears to be three separate names—Judas, Juda, Jude—the general view is that they are one in the same person. In addition, we are not informed from the scriptures the names of Jesus' sisters or the exact number. However, we know that he had at least two half sisters, perhaps more.

Based upon this knowledge, we may well suppose that if Mary had a child every two years, following the birth of our Lord, by the time she and Joseph journey to the Passover feast with Jesus, when he was twelve, she had six additional children.

As parents are aware, every child comes into this world with its own individual personality and disposition. Further, intermingling that particular child with varied-age brothers and sisters causes each sibling to react differently to a variety of situations. With younger children, it seems that at least once or several times every day, one or more child causes disharmony in the home. Also, one or more child is either sick, unhappy, hungry, or believes he or she has not been treated fairly. Since Mary and Joseph were going through mortality as other individuals, it is reasonable to believe that this mother and father experienced family life—with all of its attendant responsibilities and rewards—as other families on earth. However, because of who Jesus was, and how quickly he learned and developed spiritually, Mary and Joseph experienced parenthood differently than other parents in mortality!

Although children may be raised under one roof by the same parents, each child reacts to their parents teaching and influence unlike that of his fellow siblings. Such seems to be the case with Jesus and his half-brothers. We learn from the Apostle John that during most of our Lord's ministry, his sibling brothers did not have a testimony that he was the Savior and Redeemer of the world. The record states, "For neither did his brethren believe in him." (John 7:5) Regarding this scripture, we use the thoughts and words of Elder McConkie:

> "Frequent special reference is made to the sons of Joseph and Mary as the 'brethren' of Jesus, though in fact they were his half-brothers. (Matt. 12:46; 13:55; John 2:12; Acts 1:14; 1 Cor. 9:5) Though they were reared in the same household and came under the benign influence of Joseph and Mary, though they were aware of the teachings, ministry, and miracles of Jesus himself, yet these his close relatives had not so far accepted him as the Messiah. However, all of them, apparently, were converted later (Acts 1:14); one of them, identified by Paul as 'James the Lord's brother'(Gal. 1:19), was to minister in the holy apostleship; and yet another, Judas, who calls himself, 'Jude the...brother of James' (Jude 1), wrote the epistle of Jude."93

Regarding Jesus' half-sisters, we are not informed how they believed or if they were like unto their brothers. We can only trust that if they did not at first believe that their older brother was the Christ, they also "were converted later."

This truly was a challenging and troubling situation for Mary and Joseph to have all of Jesus' half-brothers not believe their words regarding the divinity of Jesus. As Simeon explained to her in the temple, Mary was experiencing the "sword" of grief and sorrow because of her own unconverted sons. This situation continued for nearly thirty-three years. As is the case with many good and faithful parents of disbelieving or wayward children, all that a mother or father can do is love them and sincerely pray that one day those sons or daughters will see the light and change their thinking and actions. Finally, after years of instruction, long-suffering, patience, tears, and prayer, Mary's doubting sons were converted. (*See* Acts 1:14) We do not know what caused their conversion; only that they finally became faithful and believing members. Finally, because of the conversion of her former disbelieving sons, this devoted mother experienced joy and peace of mind.

Next, we discover what happened when Jesus turned twelve.

CHAPTER TWENTY-NINE

JESUS AT TWELVE YEARS OF AGE

THE JOURNEY TO JERUSALEM

Of the four Gospels, only Luke's makes mention of the Passover feast. From his record, we discover that Joseph and Mary have gone every year to Jerusalem to celebrate the Passover. (Luke 2:41) Regarding this celebration, we use the words of Elder Talmage:

> "This religious festival, it should be remembered, was one of the most solemn and sacred among the many ceremonial commemorations of the Jews; it had been established at the time of the peoples' exodus from Egypt, in remembrance of the outstretched arm of power by which God had delivered Israel after the angel of destruction had slain the firstborn in every Egyptian home and had mercifully passed over the houses of the children of Jacob."[94]

The requirements of the law were different for men and women. As it pertains to the Passover, we use the knowledge of Frederic W. Farrar:

> "Women were, indeed, not mentioned in the law which required the annual presence of all males at the three great yearly feasts of Passover, Pentecost and Taber-

> nacles; but Mary, in pious observance of the rule recommended by Hillel, accompanied her husband every year, and on this occasion they took with them the boy Jesus, who was beginning to be of an age to assume the responsibilities of the Law."[95]

Now that Jesus was twelve years of age, it is reasonable to believe that Mary and Joseph were anxiously awaiting their yearly visit to Jerusalem. To help us better understand why Mary and Joseph especially wanted to attend this year's Passover, we again use the knowledge of Elder Talmage:

> "At twelve years of age a Jewish boy was recognized as a member of his home community; he was required then to enter with definite purpose upon his chosen vocation; he attained an advanced status as an individual in that thereafter he could not be arbitrarily disposed of as a bond-servant by his parents; he was appointed to higher studies in school and home; and, when accepted by the priests, he became a 'son of the law.' It was the common and very natural desire of parents to have their sons attend the feast of the Passover and be present at the temple ceremonies as recognized members of the congregation when of the prescribed age. Thus came the Boy Jesus to the temple."[96]

Regarding the journey to Jerusalem and the Passover observance, we paraphrase the words of Farrar on this subject. We learn that the celebration was from the end of April through the beginning of May, the observance lasting for a week. Mainly for safety reasons, large numbers of people traveled in caravans. Nazareth was a distance of about eighty miles from Jerusalem, and the time to travel was a good three days.

In addition, the number of people who came to the Passover from every region of the East might be counted by tens of thousands. These numbers were more than the city could properly accommodate in lodging. Accordingly, on the outskirts of Jerusalem, the visitors built little booths for shelter that were covered with interwoven mats and leaves. (*See The Life of Christ* pp. 36-38)

From Farrar's explanation, we can appreciate and understand better all that Mary went through in order to prepare for this three-day journey to Jerusalem; the three- or four-day stay there; and the three-day journey back to Nazareth. With the number of people in her immediate family, (counting Jesus, there may be seven children going to the Passover?) we can visualize all of the food, clothing, and bedding she packed. With Mary and Joseph taking this trip every year, we may well suppose that this wife and mother was an organized and patient person.

THE STAY IN JERUSALEM

We are not informed how long Joseph's family stayed in Jerusalem for this observance; however, based upon what Edersheim has written, it was probably no more than three or four days.

"Only on the two first days of the Feast of Passover was personal attendance in the Temple necessary. With the third day commenced...it was lawful to return to one's home...For, the Passover had been eaten..."[97]

THE JOURNEY TO NAZARETH

From Luke's Gospel, we are informed that following the conclusion of the Passover stay, and at the end of a day's journey toward Nazareth, Joseph and Mary discovered that Jesus was not with their caravan. (Luke 2:44) Some individuals may wonder how a caring and responsible mother and father would have gone that long without making sure that there son was accounted for and safe? To help answer this question, we turn to Farrar for explanation:

> "The boys and children sometimes walk and play by the side of their parents, and sometimes, when tired, get a lift on horse or mule...But, in any case, among such a sea of human beings, how easy would it be to lose one young boy!
>
> "A day elapsed before the parents discovered their loss...and all day long they would be free from anxiety, supposing that the boy was with some other group of friends or relatives in that long caravan. But when evening came, and their diligent inquiries led to no trace of Him, they would learn the bitter fact that He was altogether missing from the band of returning pilgrims."[98]

Those individuals who have been unable to find a child know of the emotions that are aroused by such a disappearance. Imagine what Mary and Joseph are feeling at this time. Continuing again with the words of Farrar, we read these poignant words:

> "The next day, in alarm and anguish—perhaps, too, with some sense of self-reproach that they had not been more faithful to their sacred charge—they retraced their steps to Jerusalem. The country was in a wild and unsettled state...This disturbed state of the political horizon would not only render their journey more difficult when once they had left the shelter of the caravan, but would

> also intensify their dread, lest, among all the wild elements of warring nationalities which at such a moment were assembled about the walls of Jerusalem, their Son should have met with harm. Truly on that day of misery and dread must the sword have pierced through the virgin mother's heart!
>
> "Neither on that day, nor during the night, nor throughout a considerable part of the third day, did they discover Him, till at last they found Him in the place which, strangely enough, seems to have been the last where they searched for him—in the Temple, 'sitting in the midst of the doctors, both hearing them and asking them questions; and all that heard Him were astonished at His understanding and answers.' [(Luke 2: 46-47)]"[99]

Let us discover what happened when Mary and Joseph found Jesus in the temple.

CHAPTER THIRTY

FINDING JESUS IN THE TEMPLE (*See* Luke 2:43-50)

Imagine the relief, joy, and wonderment of both Mary and Joseph finding Jesus alive and well, as well as hearing him conversing so impressively with the learned. We can also understand the frustration and displeasure this mother felt toward her son. As Elder Talmage has so well explained:

> "In words of gentle yet unmistakable reproof the mother said: 'Son, why has thou thus dealt with us? behold, thy father and I have sought thee sorrowing. [(Luke 2:48)]' The Boy's reply astonished them, in that it revealed, to an extent they had not before realized, His rapidly maturing powers of judgment and understanding. Said He: 'How is it that ye sought me? wist ye not that I must be about my Father's business? [(Luke 2:49)]'
>
> "Let us not say that there was unkind rebuke or unfilial reproof in the answer of this most dutiful of sons to His mother. His reply was to Mary a reminder of what she seems to have forgotten for the moment—the facts in the matter of her Son's paternity. She had used the words 'thy father and I'; and her Son's response had brought anew to her mind the truth that Joseph was not the Boy's father... He had made plain to her the inadvertent inaccuracy of her words; His Father had not been seeking Him; for was He not even at that moment in His Father's house, and partic-

ularly engaged in His Father's business, the very work to which His Father had appointed Him?

"...Interested as were the doctors in this remarkable Boy, much as He had given them to ponder over through His searching questions and wise answers, they could not detain Him, for the very law they professed to uphold enjoined strict obedience to parental authority. 'And he went down with them, and came to Nazareth, and was subject unto them....' [(Luke 2:51)]"[100]

Though Mary had been reminded who Jesus' Father was, we must not think that she ever forgot the holy experience with the "Highest." However, on this particular day in the temple, and especially after a trying three-day search for her child, this believing and loving mother did not publicly testify to the learned doctors the divinity of Jesus, but "kept all these sayings in her heart." (Luke 2:51)

THE PROPHET JOSEPH SMITH

In reference to Jesus being with the "doctors" in the temple, the Prophet Joseph Smith has revealed these great truths:

> "...but it is not always wise to relate all the truth. Even Jesus, the Son of God, had to refrain from doing so, and had to restrain His feelings many times for the safety of Himself and His followers, and had to conceal the righteous purposes of His heart in relation to many things pertaining to His Father's kingdom. When still a boy He had all the intelligence necessary to enable Him to rule and govern the kingdom of the Jews, and could reason with the wisest and most profound doctors of law and divinity, and make their theories and practice to appear like folly

compared with the wisdom He possessed; but He was a boy only, and lacked physical strength even to defend His own person; and was subject to cold, to hunger, and to death."[101]

Truly Jesus was a remarkable boy! Perhaps on other trips to the Passover, he again spoke to the learned doctors. If he spoke to them when he was twelve would he be silent until he began his formal ministry at age thirty?

JESUS APPROACHED JOHN

We advance to a time when Jesus was a grown man. Just prior to starting his formal ministry, he approached his cousin, John, and asked to be baptized. The scriptural record states, "But John forbad him, saying, I have need to be baptized of thee, and comest thou to me? And Jesus answering said unto him, Suffer it to be so now: for thus it becometh us to fulfil all righteousness. Then he suffered him." (Matt. 3:13-15)

CHRIST ORGANIZED HIS CHURCH

Following our Lord's baptism, he organized his Church and called Apostles and Prophets and other leaders, "for the perfecting of the saints, for the work of the ministry, [and] for the edifying of the body of Christ." (Eph.4:11-14) Then, as it is now, Christ's Church is the kingdom of God on earth. (D&C 35:27; 38:9, 15; 50:35; 62; 9; 136:4; *Teachings of the Prophet Joseph Smith*, pp. 271-274)

KINGDOM OF GOD

In order to receive a remission of sins, and the Holy

Ghost, a person must be baptized. (D&C 13; D&C 84:64) Further, this is the only way that a person can be admitted into the kingdom of God on earth. By being obedient to the teachings and commandments of God, which includes the necessary and important ordinance of baptism, a person can gain an inheritance in the celestial kingdom. (D&C 76:51-52, 70; 84: 64, 74)

From this explanation, we know that Christ was baptized for two important reasons: (1) to be admitted into his own Church; (2) to gain an inheritance in the celestial kingdom.

Now that we understand that it was necessary for our Lord to be baptized to "fulfill all righteousness," would it not seem reasonable to believe that Mary and Joseph would also have to be baptized? Let us explore this question in the next chapter.

CHAPTER THIRTY-ONE

WERE MARY AND JOSEPH BAPTIZED?

From the scriptures, we are not informed if Mary and Joseph were baptized. From what has been written by Edersheim, and doctrines revealed by the Lord, it is safe to assume that they were. From Edersheim, we read these informative words:

> "Hitherto the Law had it, that those who had contracted Levitical defilement were to immerse before offering sacrifice. Again, it was prescribed that such Gentiles as became 'proselytes of righteousness,' or 'proselytes of the Covenant'...were to be admitted to full participation in the privileges of Israel by the threefold rites of circumcision, baptism, and sacrifice—the immersion being, as it were, the acknowledgment and symbolic removal of moral defilement, corresponding to that of Levitical uncleanness."[102]

METHOD OF BAPTISM

He then describes how baptisms were performed back in Jesus' day:

> "The person to be baptized, having cut his hair and nails, undressed completely, made fresh profession of his

> faith before what were designated 'the fathers of the baptism'...and then immersed completely, so that every part of the body was touched by the water. The rite would, of course, be accompanied by exhortations and benedictions.
>
> "...As he stepped out of these waters he was considered as 'born anew'—in the language of the Rabbis, as if he were 'a little child just born.'...The past, with all that had belonged to it, was past, and he was a new man—the old, with its defilements, was buried in the waters of baptism."[103]

Baptism was a way of life among the faithful Jews in the day of John, known as *the Baptist.*[104] Due to apostasy and sin, not every Jewish person was baptized. However, those who looked forward to the coming of the Promised Messiah adhered to this covenant of baptism.

Mary knew and understood that John's mission was to prepare the way for Jesus, and that John would have the authority to baptize. (Matt. 3:1-5; John 1:23, 76) She learned this while visiting with Elisabeth and Zacharias. (Luke 1:76-77) With this understanding, are we amiss to believe that after Jesus was baptized that he informed his dear mother of his visit to John?

Therefore, from Edersheim's explanation, and the knowledge that Jesus was baptized by John "to fulfill all righteousness," (Matt. 3:13-15) it seems reasonable to believe that Mary and Joseph were also baptized by John.

NOTES

1. Regarding John and the authority he had to baptize, the Prophet Joseph Smith has stated: "The Levitical Priesthood

is forever hereditary...and was in active operation down to Zacharias the father of John." (*Teachings*, p. 319) Part of the function of this priesthood is the authority to baptize. (D&C 13) Again, we read: "Zacharias was a priest of God...and John was a priest after his father, and held the keys of the Aaronic Priesthood, and was called of God to preach the Gospel of the kingdom of God." (*Teachings*, p. 273) The Lord has further revealed that this same John "was baptized while he was yet in his childhood." (D&C 84:27-28) To help us understand why John was allowed to baptize, we are informed that he "was the only legal administrator in the affairs of the kingdom there was then on the earth, and the only one holding the keys of power. The Jews had to obey his instructions or be damned by their own law." (*Teachings*, p. 276) Regarding John, Luke has written: "And all the people that heard him, and the publicans, justified God being baptized with the baptism of John. But the Pharisees and lawyers rejected the counsel of God against themselves, being not baptized of him." (Luke 7:29-30) (Additional wording was added to help clarify meaning.)

CHAPTER THIRTY-TWO

MARY AT THE MARRIAGE IN CANA

Since Joseph is not mentioned being at the marriage in Cana or throughout the rest of the New Testament it is assumed that he is dead.[105] We are not informed when or how he died. We may well imagine how the death of her beloved Joseph caused Mary much sorrow and loneliness. Those who have lost a spouse know of the hardships and challenges caused by such a happening: The difficulty in raising a family alone; the many chores around the house and yard; and the financial concerns due to a decrease in income. We may safely conclude that Mary experienced all of these hardships. This truly was a sad and trying time for this widowed woman.

Regarding our Lord, it is reasonable to believe that Jesus did not live with his mother the entire thirty years prior to his ministry. Partaking of the normal Jewish life of men, as set forth by Jewish law, he must be on his own, working as a carpenter.

We may safely conclude that, since Jewish law commanded it—but more importantly because he was the Messiah—throughout Mary's widowed life, Jesus, as her oldest child, provided for her necessities and comfort. We know that when our Lord hung on the cross that he entrusted the care of his beloved mother to the Apostle John, who was a nephew of Mary. (John 19:26-27)

CANA OF GALILEE

Turning our attention to a happening in a place called Cana, we are informed, from the Gospel of John, that on the third day of the week, "there was a marriage in Cana of Galilee; and the mother of Jesus was there." (John 2:1) Further, that "Jesus was called, and his disciples, to the marriage." (John 2:2) We are not informed by whom or when Jesus and five of his new disciples were "called" and expected to be in attendance at the wedding. (John 2:1-12) We only know that they were at the wedding. It is noteworthy that our Savior's presence at this particular festivity is evidence of the divine approval of marriages and their related activities. (Heb. 13:4; Matt. 19:4-9)

Regarding this wedding, the consensus of scholars is that Mary's active part in providing for the needs of the wedding guests indicates that one of her children was being married.[106]

MARY'S REQUEST

Farrar informs us that marriage festivities could last up to a week. (*See The Life of Christ,* p.86)

According to John's record, sometime during the end of the celebration, "the mother of Jesus saith unto him, They have no wine." (John 2:3) From Mary's words, we can surmise what she expected her distinguished son to do: To provide the needed wine for the wedding guests; not by purchase, but by the use of his divine power.

RESPONSE OF JESUS

Our attention is now turned to the Messiah and his response. In unmistakable tones of authority, yet with respect, our Lord spoke these words of mild reproof: "Woman, what have I to do with thee? mine hour is not yet come." (John 2:4) From these words, we can surmise what Jesus was saying: Mother, no longer am I under your parental care or authority. I am on my Father's business, and I will determine the time and the place for performing miracles.

After receiving his reproof, Mary, because of her faith in her divine Son, knew that her request would be granted. Accordingly, she said to the servants, "Whatsoever he saith unto you, do it." (John 2:5)

"WOMAN"

Regarding Jesus calling his mother, "Woman," Elder Talmage explains:

> "The noun of address, 'Woman,' as applied by a son to his mother may sound to our ears somewhat harsh, if not disrespectful; but its use was really an expression of opposite import." In a footnote, Elder Talmage quotes the expression of Farrar: "The address 'Woman' was so respectful that it might be, and was, addressed to the queenliest."[107]

WATER TURNED INTO WINE

Jesus had the servants fill six empty waterpots full with water. Each pot held from "two or three firkins apiece" of water. (John 2:6) A firkin is equivalent to nine gallons. As soon as the containers were filled to the brim, our Lord asked those same servants to draw from a vessel and give a taste of the contents to the governor of the feast. Upon tasting the wine, this honored guest responded: "Every man at the beginning doth set forth good wine; and when men have well drunk, then that which is worse: but thou hast kept the good wine until now." (John 2:10) From the short time that the waterpots were filled with water until the servants drew it out, approximately one hundred fifty gallons of "good wine" had been produced. Whether Jesus spoke any words or simply willed it to be done, we are not informed. Whatever transpired at this event, the miracle occurred.

We can well imagine what the wedding guests said to one another upon learning from the servants how the wine was furnished. From this same record, we discover that this was the beginning of Jesus' miracles. Further, that this act "manifested forth his glory; and his disciples believed on him." (John 2:11) It should be noted that Mary's faith in her divine son caused the miracle to follow. For as we read in the Book of Mormon, "For if there be no faith among the children of men God can do no miracle among them...." (Ether 12:12)

Over the years, Mary had heard and witnessed many things concerning her divine child. Throughout these experiences, this mother had kept these things to herself. (Luke 2:19, 51) Now, at this place called Cana, and at the time of a wedding for one of her children, this believing woman has publicly demonstrated by her actions and words that she believes her divine Son is the Messiah. Mary will continue to testify that Jesus is the Christ by being one of his most faithful followers. Now, with the marriage celebration over, we shall find out why Mary goes to Capernaum.

CHAPTER THIRTY-THREE

MARY WENT TO CAPERNAUM

Following the miracle at Cana, a day or two later, Mary went with Jesus, his half-brothers, and his disciples, to the city of Capernaum. (John 2:12) Regarding this city, Elder Talmage has written:

> "...a town pleasantly situated near the northerly end of the Sea of Galilee or Lake of Gennesaret and the scene of many of our Lord's miraculous works; indeed it came to be known as His own city. Because of the unbelief of its people it became a subject of lamentation to Jesus when in sorrow He prefigured the judgment that would befall the place."[108]

In addition to Mary's loyalty in following Jesus to Capernaum, Elder McConkie has written that we may "suppose" that his mother and her sons from Joseph also resided in this town.[109] Elder McConkie's supposition seems logical since Joseph was no longer alive. It is reasonable to believe that sometime after Joseph's death, Mary disposed of the home in Nazareth and moved her family to be closer to her eldest son.

As the Passover was about to begin, we read that this small group of people "continued there not many days" in Capernaum. (John 2:12) Although the next verse states that "Jesus went up to Jerusalem," (John 2:13) it appears consistent with custom, and the preceding scripture, that all of the individuals in this group went with our Lord to observe the paschal festival together. It was at this yearly observance that our Lord, by physical force and righteous indignation, cleared the temple for the first time. (John 2:15-17) We may well believe that Mary was able to see for the first time the righteous anger of her son, and the use of his physical strength to teach all that this was his "Father's house" and that he was his Father's Son! (John 2:16)

We now turn our attention to a time when Mary desired to speak with Jesus.

CHAPTER THIRTY-FOUR

MARY DESIRED TO SPEAK WITH JESUS

Because it was so impressive, Matthew, Mark, and Luke each write of this next event. Using Matthew's words only, we read the following :

> "While he [Jesus] yet talked to the people, behold, his mother and his brethren [half-brothers] stood without, desiring to speak with him.
>
> "Then one said unto him, Behold, thy mother and thy brethren stand without, desiring to speak with thee.
>
> "But he answered and said unto him that told him, Who is my mother? and who are my brethren?
>
> "And he stretched forth his hand toward his disciples, and said, Behold my mother and my brethren!
>
> "For whosoever shall do the will of my Father which is in heaven, the same is my brother, and sister, and mother." (Matt. 12:46-50; Mark 3:31-35; Luke 8:19-21)

These words spoken by Jesus, regarding his mother and half-brothers, may appear to be inconsiderate and harsh. To help us understand these passages of scripture, we use the wisdom of Elder Talmage:

> "Making use of the circumstance to impress upon all the fact that His work took precedence over the claims of

> family and kinship, and thereby explaining that He could not meet His relatives at that moment, He asked, 'Who is my mother? and who are my brethren?...
>
> "The incident reminds one of the answer He made to His mother, when she and Joseph had found Him in the temple after their long and anxious search: 'How is it that ye sought me? wist ye not that I must be about my Father's business? [(Luke 2:49)]' In that business He was engaged when His mother and brethren desired to speak with Him as He sat admist the crowd. The superior claims of His Father's work caused Him to let all minor matters wait. We are not justified in construing these remarks as evidence of disrespect, far less of filial and family disloyalty. Devotion, similar in kind at least, was expected by Him of the apostles, who were called to devote without reserve their time and talents to the ministry. The purpose on which the relatives of Jesus had come to see Him is not made known; we may infer, therefore, that it was of no great importance beyond the family circle."[110]

We may be assured that Jesus' devotion and love for his family was strong and true. However, at this time and in this place, he had to teach and instruct while he was still on earth. In a few short years, his mortal ministry will end on the cross. We know that his mother was true to her Son and his gospel, even after Jesus' death. We can safely conclude that Mary knew that Jesus was busy preaching the gospel, and was not offended by what her divine son said to the people.

We now turn our attention to a scene of sorrow and despair—the figurative sword of grief and pain deeply piercing Mary's heart and soul.

CHAPTER THIRTY-FIVE

MARY AT JESUS' CRUCIFIXION

With the Spirit as our guide, picture our Savior hanging on the cross. On each side of him are two other people who are also being crucified. To help us fully appreciate this awful and humiliating way to be put to death, we use the skillful and moving words of Farrar:

> "The cross was not, and could not have been, the massive and lofty structure with which such myriads of pictures have made us familiar. Crucifixion was among the Romans a very common punishment, and it is clear that they would not waste any trouble in constructing the instrument of shame and torture. It would undoubtedly be made of the very commonest wood that came to hand, perhaps olive or sycamore, and knocked together in the very rudest fashion. Still, to support the body of a man, a cross would require to be of a certain size and weight; and to one enfeebled by the horrible severity of the previous scourging, the carrying of such a burden would be an additional misery. But Jesus was enfeebled not only by this cruelty, but by previous days of violent struggle and agitation, by an evening of deep and overwhelming emotion, by a night of sleepless anxiety and suffering, by mental agony of the garden, by three trials and three sentences of death before the Jews, by the long and exhausting scenes in the Praetorium, by the examination before Herod, and by the

brutal and painful derisions which He had undergone...

"The three crosses were laid on the ground—that of Jesus, which was doubtless taller than the other two, being placed in bitter scorn in the midst...He was laid down upon the implement of torture. His arms were stretched along the cross-beams, and at the [center] of the open palms the point of a huge iron nail was placed, which, by the blow of a mallet, was driven home into the wood. Then through either foot separately, or possibly through both together as they were placed one over the other, another huge nail tore its way through the quivering flesh...

"For indeed a death by crucifixion seems to include all that pain and death can have of horrible and ghastly—dizziness, cramp, thirst, starvation, sleeplessness, traumatic fever, tetanus, publicity of shame, long continuance of torment, horror of anticipation, mortification of untended wounds—all intensified just up to the point at which they can be endured at all, but all stopping just short of the point which would give to the sufferer the relief of unconsciousness. The unnatural position made every movement painful; the lacerated veins and crushed tendons throbbed with incessant anguish; the wounds, inflamed by exposure, gradually gangrened; the arteries—especially of the head and stomach—became swollen and oppressed with surcharged blood;

"...there was added to them the intolerable pang of burning and raging thirst

..."Such was the death to which Christ was doomed...

"The great body of the people seem to have stood silently at gaze; but some few of them as they passed by the cross...mocked at Jesus with insulting noises and furious taunts, especially bidding Him come down from the cross and save Himself, since He could destroy the Temple and build it in three days...

"But amid this chorus of infamy Jesus spoke not. He could have spoken. The pains of crucifixion did not confuse the intellect, or paralyze the powers of speech...

"But that silence, joined to His patient majesty and the divine holiness and innocence which radiated from Him like a halo, was more eloquent than any words...

"Though none spoke to comfort Jesus—though deep grief, and terror, and amazement kept them dumb—yet there were hearts amid the crowd that beat in sympathy with the awful Sufferer. At a distance stood a number of women looking on, and perhaps, even at that dread hour, expecting His immediate deliverance. Many of these were women who had ministered to Him in Galilee, and had come from thence in the great band of Galilean pilgrims. Conspicuous among this heart-stricken group were His mother Mary, Mary of Magdala, Mary the wife of Clopas [sic], mother of James and Joses, and Solome the wife of Zebedee. Some of them, as the hours advanced, stole nearer and nearer to the cross, and at length the filming eye of the Saviour fell on His own mother Mary, as, with the sword piercing through and through her heart, she stood with the disciple whom He loved."[111]

From these graphic and heart-rending words, we comprehend, in some degree, what Jesus' mother was feeling at seeing her Son hang on this torturous cross. Imagine the grief, torment, anguish, and helplessness she experienced hour after hour. It is without question that Mary would have done anything to have her divine son not go through this horrible ordeal. However, at this terrible time, she has not the means nor the power to relieve his suffering. Surely, by now, Mary knows that Jesus has the power to save himself; but will not.

Also, this most dutiful mother knows that Jesus came into this world to do his Father's business—he himself had reminded her of this fact when he was twelve years of age—and, even as he hangs upon the cross, he was doing the work his Father sent him to do. (Luke 2:49) Yet, being human, this grieving mother was justifiably suffering for her crucified Son. The figurative sword that Simeon had spoken of in the temple was continually piercing her heart and soul! (Luke 2:35)

From John's Gospel, we are informed that near the cross was Mary, her dear sister, Salome, Mary the wife of Cleophas, Mary Magdalene, and John, whom the Lord loved greatly. (John 19:25) In spite of all his pain and suffering, Jesus' concern was for his loving and faithful mother. With tender and caring words, our Lord said: "Woman, behold thy son! Then saith he to the disciple, Behold thy mother!" (John 19: 26-27)

DEATH OF JESUS

We are not informed if Mary actually witnessed Jesus' death, for according to his own words, John tells us that "from that hour...[he] took her unto his own home." (John 19:27)[112] We do not know exactly when Jesus died; only that it was "around 3 p.m." (Matt. 27:46)[113] Imagine the tears that were shed by Jesus' mother, as well as the other women, upon the death of our Lord. This truly was a sad and emotional time for Mary.

ENTRUSTED TO THE CARE OF JOHN (John 19:26-27)

There are four apparent reasons why Mary was entrusted

to the care of John: (1)Joseph was deceased; (2)Jesus' half-brothers had not yet been converted; (3)Mary needed association with encouraging believers; (4)John was Mary's nephew and an Apostle; he could provide for both her spiritual comfort as well as material care. We can safely suppose that Mary was well taken care of, and was blessed to be in her nephew's care for the remainder of her life, since John does not himself taste of death. (John 21:20-24; D&C 7)[114]

THE JUBILANT NEWS

After three sad days, the word was spreading that Jesus was resurrected. (Matt. 28; Mark 16; Luke 24; John 20) It is easy to comprehend the joy and wonderment Mary was feeling because of this good news! Now that the traumatic crucifixion was over, and our Lord was risen from the dead, we read of the final recorded event in Mary's life.

CHAPTER THIRTY-SIX

MARY WITH THE APOSTLES

EVENTS FOLLOWING THE RESURRECTION OF JESUS

The Gospel writers inform us that throughout his forty-day stay following his resurrection, Jesus appeared to several people. No mention is made, however, that Mary was privileged to see her resurrected Son.

From the scriptural record, we know that Mary Magdalene was the first mortal to see the resurrected Lord. (Mark 16:9-11; John 20:11-18) Afterwards, he appeared to other women: Mary the mother of Joses, to Joanna, to Salome, the mother of James and John, and to other unnamed women. (Matt. 28:1; 5-10; Mark 16:1-8; Luke 24:1-11)[115] We also know that Mary Magdalene and Mary's sister, Salome, were with Jesus' mother at the cross (John 19:25), and were the first women and individuals to see the risen Lord. By reason that Jesus appeared to these women, as well as others, is it not reasonable to believe that our Savior also appeared to his own beloved mother to give her the assurance that he was indeed resurrected?

Following our Lord's forty-day sojourn on earth as a resurrected being, the scriptural record states that Jesus finally ascended into heaven. (Acts 1:9) Regarding what transpires after this event, we again use the words of Elder Talmage:

AT A SPECIAL CHURCH MEETING

"After witnessing the Lord's ascension from Olivet, the eleven apostles returned to Jerusalem filled with joy and thoroughly suffused with the spirit of adoring worship. Both in the temple and in a certain upper room, which was their usual place of meeting, they continued in prayer and supplication, often in association with other disciples, including Mary the mother of the Lord, some of her sons, and the little sisterhood of faithful women who had ministered to Jesus in Galilee and had followed Him thence to Jerusalem and to Calvary...

"The first official act undertaken by the apostles was the filling of the vacancy in the council of the Twelve, occasioned by the apostasy and suicide of Judas Iscariot. Sometime between the ascension of Christ and the feast of Pentecost, when the Eleven and other disciples, in all about a hundred and twenty, were together...Peter laid the matter before the assembled Church,...Peter affirmed the necessity of completing the apostolic quorum; and he thus set forth the qualifications essential in the one who should be ordained to the Holy Apostleship:...Two faithful disciples were nominated by the Eleven, Joseph Barsabas and Matthias. In earnest supplication the assembly besought the Lord to indicate whether either of these men, and if so which, was to be chosen for the exalted office; then, 'they gave forth their lots; and the lot fell upon Matthias; and he was numbered with the eleven apostles.'"[116]

We are most fortunate to read that at a formal church meeting that was called to choose a new Apostle, Mary and her sons from Joseph are in attendance. From this recorded event, we can safely determine that Jesus' half-brothers were finally converted, and further, that Mary's active participation at this gathering shows that her testimony was strong and true. Also, she knows that the Apostles were duly called and set apart by her divine son, and that they collectively have the authority and inspiration to govern the affairs of her Son's Church, even The Church of Jesus Christ.

MARY'S LIFE

Following this last recorded event of Mary, we are left without knowledge of what transpired in her life. At the time of the meeting to select a new Apostle, we do not know if she was still residing with John or with one of her converted children. We also do not know how long she lived or when and how she died. We can well imagine that upon her death there was a great mourning among the members of the Church. In addition, that she was respectfully eulogized for who she was and how she lived her life.

Let us remember that she gave her all in order to serve God and his Son. Let us remember the joys, challenges, and trials she experienced being the mother of our Lord. Let us give her the respect and praise she so admirably deserves. Thanks be to Mary for being the mother of the Son of God!

"A PRECIOUS AND CHOSEN VESSEL"

In conclusion, with what is revealed in the scriptures, as well as what is written in this work, we declare with confidence that Mary truly was "a precious and chosen vessel." (Alma 7:10)

* * * * * *

Notes and Sources

In his scholarly book, *Jesus the Christ,* Elder James E. Talmage quotes from Alfred Edersheim, who was a recognized scholar who believed in Christ, and Frederic W. Farrar, who was a Biblical scholar from the Church of England. Likewise, Elder Bruce R. McConkie, in his scholarly series titled *The Mortal Messiah: From Bethlehem to Calvary,* also quotes from these same authors. To help the reader understand why Elders Talmage and McConkie quote from these noted scholars, who wrote their works over one hundred years ago, I use the words penned by Elder McConkie:

"At this point a word about almost all sectarian commentaries and biographies about Christ might not be amiss. It is my judgment that most of the modern publications are far from faith promoting. In most cases it is necessary to go back a hundred years or so to find authors who believed in the divine Sonship with sufficient fervor to accept the New Testament passages as meaning what they say. . ." *(The Mortal Messiah: From Bethlehem to Calvary, Book 4, p. 425, note 2.)*

He further writes:

"I have not hesitated to quote selected literary gems and to paraphrase others,... throughout this work, with particular reference to the writings of Edersheim and Farrar, two of the best sectarian authors.. ." (Ibid., Book 2, p 339, note 2.)

In addition, Elder McConkie writes these praising words about the book, *Jesus the Christ:*

". . . . I have a deep and profound respect for *Jesus the Christ,* the scholarly work of Elder James E. Talmage, one of my most prominent predecessors. (Ibid,Book 1, Preface, p. xvii.)

In my judgment, other than the Prophet Joseph Smith, Elder Bruce R. McConkie is the premier doctrinal authority in the Church. His literary talents and doctrinal knowledge is well-known by the members of the Church. It is my prayer that all members of the Church will read and study the writings of this mighty apostolic witness of the Lord.

With this introduction, the references for each chapter will be listed.

Chapter One

1. Regarding Spirits looking like mortals, *See* the author's book, *Mysteries of the Kingdom,* Cedar Fort, Inc., 2001, pp. 53-62.

2. Regarding the time spent in the premortal existence, the reader is again referred to *Mysteries of the Kingdom,* pp. 88-90.

3. Bruce R. McConkie, *The Mortal Messiah: From Bethlehem to Calvary,* Book I, Note 4. (Salt Lake City: Deseret Book, 1979) pp. 326-327. Used by permission.

4. Bruce R. McConkie, Council of the Twelve, an address, June 29, 1978, at the dedication Services at Nauvoo. pp. 3-5; ("Source of quote") Copyright The Church of Jesus Christ of Latter-day Saints. Used by permission.

Chapter Two

5. Alfred Edersheim, *The Life and Times of Jesus the Messiah.* Eighth Printing, Revised. 1896. Original printing was in 1883. In two volumes. Throughout this book, his work will be referred to as Edersheim. Please see note 1 at the end of the chapter.

6. Bruce R. McConkie, *The Mortal Messiah: From Bethlehem to Calvary,* Book 1 (Salt Lake City: Deseret Book, 1979), pp. 217-218. Used by permission.

7. *Sketches of Jewish Social Life in the Days of Christ,* 1876. p. 123.

8. Bruce R. McConkie, *The Mortal Messiah: From Bethlehem to Calvary,* Book 1 (Salt Lake City: Deseret Book, 1979), p. 218. Used by permission.

9. Ibid., p. 219.

10. Ibid. p. 219-220.

Chapter Three

11. Edersheim, Book 1, p. 228.

12. Ibid., p. 228.

13. Ibid., p. 228.

14. Ibid., p. 228.

15. The Torah is the complete body of Jewish religious law and learning.

16. Sages are recognized Jewish men of distinction and wisdom.

17. Edersheim, Book 1, p. 230.

Chapter Four

18. Edersheim, Book 1, p. 230.

19. Ibid., p. 232. See note 1 and 2 at the end of the chapter.

20. Ibid., p. 232.

21. Bruce R. McConkie, *The Mortal Messiah: From Bethlehem to Calvary,* Book 1 (Salt Lake City: Deseret Book, 1979), pp. 42-43. Used by permission.

Chapter Five

22. For a more thorough study on this subject, the reader is referred to the author's book, *Mysteries of the Kingdom,* Cedar Fort, Inc., 2001, pp. 53-62.

Chapter Six

23. James E. Talmage, *Jesus the Christ,* 1962 edition. Original printing, 1915.

24. Edersheim, Book 2, p. 602.

25. Bruce R. McConkie, *The Mortal Messiah: From Bethlehem to Calvary,* Book 4 (Salt Lake City: Deseret Book, 1981), p. 223. Used by permission.

Chapter Seven

26. Edersheim, Book 1, p. 146.

27. Ibid., Book 1, pp. 146-148.

28. Bruce R. MeConkie, *The Mortal Messiah: From Bethlehem to Calvary,* Book 1 (Salt Lake City: Deseret Book, 1979), p. 316. Used by permission.

Chapter Eight

29. *See* note 1 at the end of chapter.

30. Frederic W. Farrar, *The Life of Christ.* Burt's Library of the World's Best Books. No date. p. 36. Original printing of London: Cassell & Co., Ltd., 1874. Throughout this book, his work will be referred to as Farrar.

31. Quoted in his work, *Sketches of Jewish Social Life in the Days of Christ,* p. 105, as printed in Bruce R. McConkie, *The Mortal Messiah: From Bethlehem to Calvary,* Book 1 (Salt Lake City: Deseret Book, 1979), p. 227.

32. Bruce R. McConkie, *The Mortal Messiah: From Bethlehem to Calvary,* Book 1 (Salt Lake City: Deseret Book, 1979), p. 223. Used by permission.

33. Ibid., Book 1, p. 227, note 4. Used by permission.

Chapter Nine

34. James E. Talmage, *Jesus the Christ,* 1962, p. 89, note 4.

35. Edersheim, Book 1, pp. 149-150.

36. See note 1 at end of chapter.

37. James E. Talmage, *Jesus the Christ,* 1962, p. 80.

38. Ibid., p. 81.

Chapter Ten

39. This is a figurative statement. Angels and spirit beings do not have wings. See Joseph Fielding Smith, comp., *Teachings of the Prophet Joseph Smith,* 1938, p. 162.

40. Bruce R. McConkie, *The Mortal Messiah. From Bethlehem to Calvary,* Book 1 (Salt Lake City: Deseret Book, 1979) , pp. 413-414.

41. Elder Melvin J. Ballard, *The Three Degrees of Glory*. A discourse given at the Ogden Tabernacle, September 22, 1922, p. 10. Regarding this doctrine, See the author's book, *Mysteries of the Kingdom,* Cedar Fort, Inc., 2001, pp. 63-64.

42. Charles W. Penrose, *Mormon Doctrine, Plain and Simple, or, Leaves from the Tree of Life*. Published 1888, p. 44. *See* also *Mysteries of the Kingdom,* pp. 63-64.

43. James E. Talmage, *Jesus the Christ,* 1962, p. 81.

Chapter Eleven

44. Joseph Fielding Smith, comp., *Teachings of the Prophet Joseph Smith,* 1938, p. 190.

45. First Article of Faith.

46. *See* note 1 at end of chapter.

47. Heber C. Kimball, *Journal of Discourses,* Volume 8, p. 211, September 2, 1860. See the author's book, *Mysteries of the Kingdom,* Cedar Fort, Inc., 2001, p. 20.

48. Brigham Young, *Journal of Discourses,* Volume 8, p. 115, July 8, 1860. *See* the author's book, *Mysteries of the Kingdom,* pp. 20-21.

49. Bruce R. McConkie, *Mormon Doctrine,* 2nd ed., Bookcraft, 1966, 1986. Copyright 1966, 1986 by Bookcraft, Inc. p. 547. Used by permission. *See* the author's book, *Mysteries of the Kingdom,* p. 21.

50. Ibid., p. 742. *See* the author's book, *Mysteries of the Kingdom,* p. 21.

Chapter Twelve

51. Bruce R. McConkie, *Doctrinal New Testament Commentary, Volume 1: The Gospels,* Bookcraft, 1965. Copyright 1965 by Bookcraft, Inc., pp. 82-83. Used by permission.

52. Ibid., p. 82. Used by permission.

Chapter Thirteen

53. Bryant S. Hinckley, *Sermons and Missionary Services of Melvin Joseph Ballard* (Salt Lake City: Deseret Book, 1949), pp. 166-167. Used by permission.

Chapter Fourteen

54. Orson Pratt, Council of the Twelve, *The Seer,* Washington D.C. Edition, October, 1853, p. 158.

55. Ibid., November, 1853, p. 172.

56. Brigham Young, *Journal of Discourses,* Volume 11, p. 268, August 19, 1866. See the author's book, *Mysteries of the Kingdom,* p. 29.

57. President Joseph F. Smith, an address given at Box Elder Stake Conference, December 20, 1914; printed in the *Box Elder News* of January 28, 1915. *See* the author's book, *Mysteries of the Kingdom,* pp. 29-30.

Chapter Fifteen

58. Bruce R. McConkie, *The Mortal Messiah: From Bethlehem to Calvary,* Book 1 (Salt Lake City: Deseret Book, 1979), p. 322. Used by permission.

Chapter Sixteen

59. Bruce R. McConkie, *The Mortal Messiah: From Bethlehem to Calvary,* Book 1, (Salt Lake City: Deseret Book, 1979), p. 319. Used by permission.

60. Ibid., Book 1, p. 333.

61. Edersheim, Book 1, p. 149.

62. James E. Talmage, *Jesus the Christ*, 1962, p. 82.

63. Bruce R. McConkie, *The Mortal Messiah: From Bethlehem to Calvary*, Book 1, (Salt Lake City: Deseret Book, 1979) pp. 320; 331-332.

64. See Chapter Twenty-Three in this book.

Chapter Seventeen

65. Joseph Fielding Smith, comp., *Teachings of the Prophet Joseph Smith*, 1938, p. 328.

66. James E. Talmage, *Jesus the Christ*, 1962, p. 83.

67. Ibid., p. 83.

68. Wording taken from *Jesus the Christ*, 1962, p. 83.

Chapter Eighteen

69. Bruce R. McConkie, *The Mortal Messiah: From Bethlehem to Calvary*, Book 1 (Salt Lake City: Deseret Book, 1979), pp. 331-332. Used by Permission.

70. Edersheim, Book 1, p. 155.

Chapter Nineteen

71. Edersheim, Book 1, pp. 354-355.

Chapter Twenty

72. James E. Talmage, *Jesus the Christ*, 1962, pp. 91-92.

73. Bruce R. McConkie, *The Mortal Messiah: From Bethlehem to Calvary*, Book 1, (Salt Lake City: Deseret Book, 1979), p. 341.

74. Farrar, p. 4.

75. Ibid., pp. 4-5.

Chapter Twenty-One

76. Farrar, p.3.

Chapter Twenty-Two

77. James E. Talmage, *Jesus the Christ,* 1962, p. 93.

78. Ibid., p. 94.

79. Farrar, p. 7.

Chapter Twenty-Three

80. James E. Talmage, *Jesus the Christ,* 1962, p. 95.

81. Ibid., p. 95.

82. Ibid., pp. 95-96.

83. Edersheim, Book 1, p. 193.

84. James E. Talmage, *Jesus the Christ,* 1962, p. 96.

Chapter Twenty-Four

85. James E. Talmage, *Jesus the Christ,* 1962, p. 97.

Chapter Twenty-Five

86. Farrar, pp. 8-9.

87. Bruce R. McConkie, *The Mortal Messiah: From Bethlehem to Calvary,* Book 1 (Salt Lake City: Deseret Book, 1979), pp. 356-357. Used by permission.

88. Edersheim, Book 1, pp. 207-208.

Chapter Twenty-Six

89. Farrar, p. 19.

90. James E. Talmage, *Jesus the Christ,* 1962, p. 110.

91. Ibid., p. 111.

Chapter Twenty-Seven

92. The reading of three passages of scriptures from Deuteronomy 6: 4-9; 11: 13-21, and Numbers 15:37-41. These passages expressed the basic belief of Jews concerning the Lord.

Chapter Twenty-Eight

93. Bruce R. McConkie, *Doctrinal New Testament Commentary, Volume 1: The Gospels*, Bookcraft, 1965. Copyright 1965 by Bookcraft, Inc., p. 437. Used by permission.

Chapter Twenty-Nine

94. James E. Talmage, *Jesus the Christ*, 1962, p. 112.

95. Farrar, p. 36.

96. James E. Talmage, *Jesus the Christ*, 1962, p. 113.

97. Edersheim, Book 1, p. 246.

98. Farrar, pp. 38-39.

99. Ibid., p. 39.

Chapter Thirty

100. James E. Talmage, *Jesus the Christ*, 1962, pp. 114-115.

101. Joseph Fielding Smith, *Teachings of the Prophet Joseph Smith*, 1968, p. 392. *See* the author's book, *Mysteries of the Kingdom*, pp. 31-32.

Chapter Thirty-One

102. Edersheim, Book 1, p. 273.

103. Ibid., Book 2, pp. 745-746.

104. See note 1 and 2 at end of chapter.

Chapter Thirty-Two

105. Edersheim, Book 1, p. 356; Farrar, p. 86; Bruce R. McConkie, *The Mortal Messiah,* Book 1, pp. 448-449.

106. Regarding the marriage in Cana, the reader is referred to the author's book, *Mysteries of the Kingdom,* pp. 33-41.

107. James E. Talmage, *Jesus the Christ,* 1962, p. 144.

Chapter Thirty-Three

108. James E. Talmage, *Jesus the Christ.* 1962, p. 153.

109. Bruce R. McConkie, *The Mortal Messiah: From Bethlehem to Calvary,* Book 1 (Salt Lake City: Deseret Book, 1979), p. 455.

Chapter Thirty-Four

110. James E. Talmage, *Jesus the Christ,* 1962, pp. 272-273.

Chapter Thirty-Five

111. Farrar, pp. 493-504.

112. See also Bruce R. McConkie, *The Mortal Messiah: From Bethlehem to Calvary,* Book 4, (Salt Lake City: Deseret Book, 1981), p. 234.

113. Ibid., p. 224.

114. Bruce R. McConkie, *Doctrinal New Testament Commentary, Volume 1; The Gospels,* Bookcraft, 1965, p. 826.

Chapter Thirty-Six

115. Bruce R. McConkie, *The Mortal Messiah: From Bethlehem to Calvary,* Book 4, (Salt Lake City: Deseret Book, 1981), p. 265. *See* also *Doctrinal New Testament Commentary: Volume 1, The Gospels.* Bookcraft, 1965, p. 846.

116. James E. Talmage, *Jesus the Christ,* 1962, pp. 700-701.

INDEX

About the Author

Bruce E. Dana is an avid student of the gospel, who served as a missionary in the Northwestern States and Pacific Northwest missions for the Church. He attended Weber State College and Utah State University. He has served in a wide variety of Church callings and enjoys teaching the doctrines of the gospel. He is married to Brenda Lamb and is the father of eight children.

Bruce is the author of nine published LDS doctrinal books. They are *Mysteries of the Kingdom*; *Mary, Mother of Jesus*; *Simon Peter*; *The Three Nephites and Other Translated Beings*; *Glad Tidings Near Cumorah*; *The Eternal Father and His Son*; *The Apostleship*; *The Three Most Important Events: The Vital Roles of the Creation, the Fall and the Atonement in Our Lives; Prophetic Teachings on Death, Angels, and Heavenly Manifestations;* and the bestselling humor book *Stories & Jokes of Mormon Folks.*

0 26575 10421 9